105L
my+
8.65

Tales
of TICASUK

Tales of TICASUK

Eskimo legends & stories

Collected and written by
Emily Ivanoff Brown "Ticasuk"

Illustrated by
Eugene C. and Mary Lou Totten

University of Alaska Press
Fairbanks

Elmer E. Rasmuson Library Cataloging-in-Publication Data

Ticasuk, 1904-
    Tales of Ticasuk: Eskimo legends and stories.

    1. Eskimos—Legends. I. Title

E99.E7T544 1984
                                        87-081286
ISBN: 0-912006-45-5

Typesetting by the University of Alaska Fairbanks
Printing and Duplicating Services.
Printed in the United States by Thomson-Shore, Inc.

This publication was printed on acid-free paper which meets the
minimum requirements of American National Standard for Information
Sciences—Permanence of Paper for Printed Library Materials.
ANSI Z39.48-1984.

Publication coordination, design and production by Deborah Van Stone.

Cover illustration by Eugene C. and Mary Lou Totten.
Cover design by Cathy Cunningham.
Cartography by Don Haas.

DEDICATED TO

my grandchildren and
all the school children who
will enrich their heritage as
they read and learn about
the Eskimo Stories

Contents

List of Illustrations

Publisher's Note

Preparing a book of legends for publication is sufficient to occupy the energies of a press; when the author herself is something of a legend, the task snowballs. How can one do justice to the unique voice of Emily Ivanoff Brown? She was a vocal bridge between two of Alaska's cultures, the new and the old; a devout Christian who was passionately concerned that the old tales of the shamans not be lost; a determined student of the linguistics of her people and of American journalism who was also a feisty lady quite willing to disagree with her teachers. All this comes through in her renderings of the ancient tales and her writing of contemporary ones, and these many tones within the one authorial voice provide a challenge indeed.

For example: in the Norton Sound area, both Unaliq (the northern dialect of central Alaskan Yupik Eskimo) and Inupiaq (northern Eskimo) are spoken. The stories in this book contain words and phrases from both languages; the languages not only have some different sounds—as much, say, as French and Spanish—but they are also represented today by different writing systems. Attempting to honor as much as possible Emily Brown's wish to spell these words so an English-speaker could read them while yet trying to indicate some of the special quality of the sounds, we have arrived at one spelling system for these stories that uses a minimum of diacritical marks or startling spellings. The letter q, for instance, represents the back-k, the sound of k made far back in the mouth. An ordinary-looking r in the Eskimo words represents the back-r sound, one that would come more naturally to speakers of French or Danish; the ř symbolizes an r-like sound pronounced near the front of the mouth. The letter combination hl indicates a voiceless l, a whispered sound off the sides of the tongue; x is a voiceless k. We owe great thanks to Lawrence Kaplan of the Alaska Native Language Center for assisting us in devising an orthography that permits both Eskimo languages to be presented in a reasonably consistent spelling system. To him should go great credit for the features of this system that work, but no blame for the ones that do not; we insisted upon compromises he would not have chosen.

Others also helped convey the unique world of Ticasuk to a wider world of readers north and south. We thank K. Fiedler Morack for her "light-handed editing," as she put it, and book design assistance. We are also most grateful to the illustrators, Eugene C. and Mary Lou Totten, who worked with Emily and her stories to create a set of visions to illuminate her views.

Finally, special thanks go to Jimmy Bedford for his work with Emily on the manuscript. Without Mr. Bedford, this book could not have been published.

University of Alaska Press

Notes on the Author

Of all the legends collected over the years by Ticasuk, none are more interesting than the true story of the incredible journey through life of Emily Ivanoff Brown.

It all began February 21, 1904, in Unalakleet where she was born to Amelia (Malquay) and Stephan Ivanoff. He was a Russian-American-Eskimo boatbuilder, skilled carpenter, storekeeper, and Covenant church missionary.

Emily's Eskimo name, Ticasuk, means "a hollow place in the ground" where the four winds store the treasure they gathered from all parts of the world; and Emily spent her lifetime serving as a focal point where people and ideas could find a place to get together.

Emily's parents built a roadhouse at Unalakleet, "well patronized by the mail carriers who travelled the North in winter by dog sled," she wrote in her book *Roots of Ticasuk*, published in 1981 by Alaska Northwest Publishing Company. Unfortunately, the prosperity they earned through their hard work was not appreciated in the village. "The chief said that they had broken the community taboo that 'no member of our village will rise in wealth over and beyond the others'," Emily was told.

The Ivanoffs sold their business "to a white man" and moved with their three sons and 3-year-old Emily to Shaktoolik, farther along the shore of Norton Sound. It was here at Shaktoolik that Emily began her education in a tent, beginning in the spring of 1909 at the age of 5.

She grew up on the cutting edge of two civilizations. Her mother clung to the old ways of the Eskimo heritage, while Stephan held to the culture of the white man's ways.

When she was about 15, she was sent to Chemawa Indian School in Salem, Oregon, where she remained for 9 years. She was there so long that the other students often called her "Grandma," but in the process of learning, she received her elementary, high school, and teaching certificate, enabling her to return to Alaska as a teacher in the school at Kotzebue.

Although she enjoyed teaching, Ticasuk was appalled at the health hazards in the villages and she decided to become a nurse. She went back to the Pacific Northwest to study nursing in Seattle.

Her nursing career was cut short when she met and married Robert Brown and the couple returned to Alaska where they had three children. Emily's new vocation as a mother was interrupted when her husband died, and she had to return to teaching to support herself and her three sons.

In 1954, at the age of 50, Emily began 10 years of attending summer school at the university to earn her bachelor of science degree in education while teaching full time during the academic years.

By May 22, 1964, when she received her degree, one would think that Ticasuk would have had enough education, but she immediately plowed into another course to study the visually handicapped child.

She continued taking courses every summer even after she retired from 30 years of teaching. Still, she studied on, after her three sons were grown and making their own living.

Emily's thirst for knowledge was so great that in the fall of 1969 she moved onto the campus at the University of Alaska in Fairbanks and stayed there through each academic year until her death on May 3, 1982.

During her last semester, she was enrolled in an individual study course in Eskimo heritage, but ill health was catching up with her and she spent very few days in her room at 104 Wickersham Hall. Most of her spring semester in Fairbanks she spent at Fairbanks Memorial Hospital, except for two trips home to Unalakleet.

In late March 1982, she flew to Anchorage to attend the Alaskan of the Year dinner where she was to receive the governor's award for outstanding service to her fellow Alaskans. Unfortunately, she was too tired to go to the dinner and her granddaughter, Paula, accepted the award for her.

Emily's service to her state was widely known and she received many awards throughout her lifetime, including a presidential citation by Richard Nixon for her "exceptional service to others, in the finest American tradition."

She was twice cited by the Alaska legislature for preservation of Alaska Native culture. This included her involvement in the production of a dictionary for her own Malimiut dialect of the Inupiaq Eskimo language. She was also assisting in the development of a curriculum guide for teaching the Inupiaq language and culture in the elementary schools.

Her teaching career included schools at Kotzebue, Unalakleet, Shaktoolik and Meade River. After returning from teaching, she was widely sought as a speaker or resource person for conferences throughout the state.

At the same time, she continued her schooling, learning more about Native language, arts, and culture, and concentrated on writing these things down for her own people and to communicate their heritage to other cultures.

Her many projects were carried out in spite of difficult battles with tuberculosis, cancer, cataracts, and other health problems. She continued to earn degrees. In 1973 she completed the master of arts degree in communication arts. In 1980 she was graduated again, with a bachelor of arts in Inupiaq Eskimo, then enrolled again to begin work on a Ph.D.

Eventually, her poor health began to catch up with her. A year before she died, a doctor predicted she would not survive more than three months—but he didn't tell Emily.

She said at the time of her return from the intensive care unit that "I've been cured." Whether she was cured or not, there seemed to be some kind of remission of the cancer and by August she was ready for another year of school. When I went to Unalakleet to visit her that month, she asked me, "When does school start?"

After learning the dates, she asked "When is our weekly conference?"

"Conference?" I asked. "I've retired, Emily. This was my last year of teaching. I'm back working as a journalist again."

"Retired! You're too young to retire. Even if you retire from the university, you can't retire from the book publishing ventures we've been working on. Now tell me, when will we have our weekly conference?"

"Well," I said resignedly, "let me see your course schedule after you're enrolled and we'll work out a suitable time."

Although she was very tired from her longtime struggle just to stay alive and she sometimes needed blood transfusions to give her strength, she continued to move about the campus, though ever so slowly now, moving ahead on her manuscripts in spite of eyes that were so weak that reading was nearly impossible. In December, there was some improvement in her eyes after a cataract operation on one eye and a laser operation in the other, but her general condition was deteriorating.

On April 15, after a two-week rest at Unalakleet with her oldest son, Leonard, and his family, Emily returned to Fairbanks Memorial Hospital. When I stopped in to see her a few days later, Emily was resigned: "I'm not going to make it this time," she said. "Let's get busy. We have much work to do before I go. First off, I've got to get new glasses so I can see to read. Will you take me to the doctor tomorrow?"

Deeply religious, Emily had long ago made peace with her God. When I took her in a wheelchair to the doctor, her mind was racing through images of work that needed to be done, vacation plans she knew would never be carried out, and her imminent death. "Don't cry at my funeral," she said. "It should be a happy time because I'm going to be with the Lord."

After a brief pause, she began to talk about summer plans and asked me to come to Unalakleet in early June to photograph several plants for a section of the Eskimo encyclopedia she was planning. "My niece and I are going to set up a big tent at Unalakleet, over by the trees, but away from the bears. We'll put it where we can hear the birds singing in the morning. My niece will cut the wood and do the heavy work and I'll do the cooking."

A week later she was sinking fast. She whispered to me "I'm going to Heaven." Five days later she was gone. She would not live to receive her doctorate.

"I am overwhelmed!" she had written Chancellor Patrick O'Rourke, upon receiving notice she would become an honorary doctor of humanities. "This news has uplifted my spirits, especially to try to continue to live to complete the work on the Eskimo encyclopedia and to promote building a multicultural center on the Fairbanks campus."

Son Melvin Brown, a 1967 graduate of the university, accepted the doctorate for her on May 9. Although Emily didn't live to see all her goals accomplished, she died knowing that others would carry on her work.

Besides her published works, she left five manuscripts to be edited for posthumous publication; this is the first to reach the presses. The others are a book of Eskimo songs, a book of poetry, a biography of her oldest son, and her life's story, which she wrote collaborating with P.M. Ivey who is completing the work. Contributions to assist with projects may be made through the University of Alaska Foundation.

She left behind her three sons: Leonard of Unalakleet; Stanley of California; and Melvin of Anchorage; nine grandchildren; and one great-granddaughter.

Finally, Emily would be pleased to know that these legends — each of which teaches a valuable moral — would be published by her own alma mater, through the University of Alaska Press, which was just beginning to roll about the time she entered the University to complete — no, not complete, but to further her education. She was still learning as she was drawing her last breath on this earth.

Jimmy Bedford

Foreword

I first met Emily Brown during a visit to the University of Alaska at Fairbanks where, as a grandmother, she was also a student. It was impossible not to be drawn to her—to that disarmingly broad, gentle smile that radiated from her face; to that childlike fascination with all that was going on around her; to the way she gestured with her arms and hands as she warmed to new acquaintances and began to tell stories with one hand sometimes balled into a fist and thrust through the air before her in determination, or both hands open, palms down, rising and falling together in graceful approximation of an umiak on the waves. It was as fascinating to watch her talk as it was to listen to what she was saying. And it was wonderful to listen, enjoying not only the quiet power of her narrative but also the way she studded her sentences with Native names and words—umiak, ugřuk, ulu—each defined for the benefit of people like myself, causing me, as their cadences (polished, practiced and as smooth as Ohio buckeyes) became wedged in my mind, to allow myself to believe that I was being welcomed into a private, almost confidential, world.

It was only after I had known her for several days that I realized that much of what drove this deceptively self-effacing woman was fueled by resentment and frustration. In the main, this was rightfully directed toward white missionaries and the authors of directives from the U.S. Office of Education, all of which seemed designed to destroy the Eskimo culture that had nourished and shaped Emily's soul. As a 15-year-old student at a BIA boarding school in the lower forty-eight, for example, she was forbidden to speak her Native language. Back in Alaska, now as a teacher, she and her peers were admonished to punish any of their students who did likewise, even in play at recess. All teaching materials, all texts, all conversation: all English. And from missionaries came similar constraints: all Native religious practices and all legends and beliefs were to be replaced by Christian doctrine. At the conclusion of the legend of the baby ogre in this volume, there is a telling line: "And when the Gospel came, the crying ceased forever."

In the face of this perceived injustice, Emily began a wise and wonderful quest. Rather than waiting for white anthropologists to salvage what was left of the culture after years of abuse, she began to do something about it herself. She began, for example, to help teach Native students their own language again, fretting over their clumsy, childlike mispronunciations of the words that belonged to them. She began to interview Native informants, some of whom were family members, to learn the legends that had not been taught to her by her mother when she was a girl. And she began to write, carefully committing to paper in book-length manuscripts such things as the legends she collected, her own autobiography, and Eskimo songs. She also assisted in the production of a dictionary of her own Eskimo dialect, and began work on an Eskimo encyclopedia (which is as yet uncompleted).

The stunning contribution she left behind at her death in 1982 does not represent all she had hoped to accomplish. She always had more projects underway than she could complete; could she have been given a second, equally long lifetime, the same situation would also exist at its conclusion. But what she did accomplish is remarkable, standing as a shining example for others, not only of her own culture but also of cultures worldwide, to build on and emulate.

This book, then, now takes its place beside her other works. Its primary audience was intended by her to be Eskimo children—the rightful heirs of its contents—and I hope this book will find that audience. Knowing Emily, however, I feel sure that that radiant smile would cross her face if she felt that others of us, too, were enjoying it, for it is a gift from her to all of us, gratefully received and savored.

Eliot Wigginton

Introduction
and
Acknowledgments

The Unaliq Folktales

The Unaliq-speaking Eskimos, the Unalit, once inhabited the coastal regions of Bering Sound and part of the Bering Sea extending from Unalakleet, Alaska, the southern boundary, and as far northwest as Uqpiktulik, now an ancient unmarked village site on the coast halfway between Nome and Golovnin Bay on the Seward Peninsula.

Historically, all the Eskimo villages in this vicinity were named by the Unaliq-speaking people. Remnants of other old Eskimo villages still exist in this area. The Unalit usually identify these sites by a statement such as "Our ancestors lived here, once."

To reinforce their description, they often tell a legend to convey how this particular village became extinct. Some people may wonder how the Eskimos can verify such statements as facts.

One such proof is connected with the names of the old existing villages. All have been named in the Unaliq language. Furthermore, the older people usually give similar background information concerning the Unalit and their settlements in a particular country. When the northern Eskimos moved southward, some settled in Unalakleet, Alaska. However, there is no reference available as to how they were accepted by the chief of the indigenous Unalit. According to the Inupiat's or northern tribes' history, they formed their own chieftain system of government. It was at this period that the Unalit named the Inupiat, "Malimiut." As a result of the friendly relationship, their children intermarried and a new generation was born. By this union the folktales, art, music, and crafts were preserved, even to the present time.

Ancient villages of the Unalit are located at Shaktoolik, north of Unalakleet on Norton Sound; Ayaatayat and Nukleet on the Cape Denbigh peninsula north of Shaktoolik on the other side of Norton Bay; Ikngittuq on the west side of Rocky Point on the Bering Sea; and Uqpiktulik west of Ikngiituq. Uqpiktulik is the terminal village of the Unalit settlements, according to Mrs. Minnie Tucker, one of our oldest Eskimo women, who was born in the 1860s in a small village on the Bering Sea coast.

The most famous and the oldest site is at Ayaatayat, Cape Denbigh. Carbon-14 dating has revealed that this site is 6,000 to 10,000 years old. Some of the oldest legends and myths known to us are Makka-tahlungiq ("Ogre Baby"); Eagle-men, the Cliff-Dwellers; Giant Travel-ler; How Mischievous Boys Were Killed; How Orphan Boy Destroys an Eskimo Village; and Qatqazaggaq or, as it is sometimes called, Ihlliaraq.

Basically, the same folktale themes are known by the northern and southern Eskimos, but the settings, characters, and dialects have been changed to parallel their own philosophies or to fit the patterns of their cultures. This procedure might have evolved from sharing their oral literature during the annual festivals in the historical past.

This writer's mother, Malrui or "Malquay," stated that preparations for coming celebrations were very elaborate. The host participants were made to practice nightly in the council house, or qařgi. During the last rehearsal, if a group of singers, individual performers, or storytellers made an error, that act or song was erased from the list as discarded material. However, it could be used the following year.

Every able member of the community took part in cmmunal cele-brations, since our Eskimo culture is basically a noncompetitive soci-ety. The children also performed. My mother, at the age of 6, was taught how to perform for the audience by doing an interpretive dance. The theme of this dance and its motif was presented so the audience would interpret how Malquay's ancestors made their living. Her ancestors were traders and they exchanged their products with the Eskimos who lived in other areas. They travelled by boat. Hence, my mother conveyed, in her act, the art of sailing in the umiak (skin boat).

A Word About Spelling

The Eskimo languages were not written until the missionaries and linguists came to communicate. In the process of putting the sounds on paper, our 26-letter English alphabet is a bit hard pressed sometimes to get it right, and so the linguists added special markings such as little circles over some letters to show that they are different from English and used the letter q as well as k to better show the special kinds of sounds the Eskimos make that are not exactly ks, but are similar.

Because many of the readers of this book are not linguists or speakers of Yupik or Inupiaq, some compromises were made. We use a q for the back-k sound and eliminate the special alphabetical markings.*

In some cases, place names will be spelled a little differently than those on the map, reflecting the author's efforts to more exactly duplicate the proper Eskimo pronunciation.

Acknowledgments

First of all I am grateful to my parents, Stephan and Amelia Malquay Ivanoff, who loved and led their children to understand the concept of education. My mother's unique ability to tell Eskimo folktales, and even to instill them in our memory, has bequeathed to us some of the most ancient legends and myths. I have included them in this collection. My father, a true genius, taught his children the

*The editors tried, but had to use one diacritical mark. See Publisher's Note.

values of life, such as creativity and the use of time, the love of God, and respect for work.

When I was very young, my mother began telling folktales, and my brothers and I also learned to tell these stories. Sometimes my Eskimo aunts or grandfathers would tell Unaliq-type stories. We loved to hear them because they stirred the imagination. They also told us stories about our culture.

Always at bedtime, even when I was only 3 years old, my mother would tell me the very same story again and again. It was a ritual, really. I never grew tired of listening to it. Her motive was to teach me to listen and to absorb the story until I could retell it to her.

Although my parents had been introduced to the white culture during my childhood, they taught us to respect the values of both cultures. Out of whatever was deposited in my mind, I eventually developed this art of story telling. When I became an elementary school teacher, this talent was useful to me in my work with the school children.

I have travelled the cross-cultural road "on foot" all my life, and I doubt whether I will ever reach the perfect usage of the English language. Here, I wish to express my deepest appreciation to my English professor, Mr. Charles J. Keim, whose first name is not Charlie, but Charles and I'm glad that it is. He is a most untiring, dedicated teacher. He feels what his students' destinies can be.

I am grateful to the many Native storytellers who showed me unselfishness, love, and friendship. Some of these people are: my aunt Abigail Kiiriq Eveb of Shaktoolik; Mrs. Frieda Goodwin of Kotzebue; Mrs. Amak Newsik of Unalakleet; Mrs. Minnie Tucker of Fairbanks; Mrs. Ruth Harris of Kotzebue; Abraham Lincoln (not the 16th President) also of Kotzebue whose father, Nasuk, was a widely known storyteller and who made it possible for me to write the legend of Kotzebue; my aunt Kiatcha, who taught me the story about the camprobber bird before Christmas so I could tell the story to an audience; and Mrs. Daisy Shugluk of Barrow. I also thank Professor Oliver Everette, who clarified the essence of poetry writing, and another friend, Dorothy Jean Ray, Eskimo stylist, anthropologist, and writer, who helped with my manuscript.

Finally, I owe my education to my Alma Mater, the University of Alaska, its professors and secretaries, who gave me guidance when I was stumbling over many jawbreakers in the English language. And special thanks to Mrs. Maurice Langhorne who typed the manuscript, and Professor Jimmy Bedford who helped with the final editing. I owe them all a "quyanaqpak (big thank you)."

Emily Ivanoff Brown
"Ticasuk"

Tales
of TICASUK

Mythology of Ayaatayat

Ayaatayat, the original village at Cape Denbigh, is the grandfather of all the Eskimo villages in that area. It was the very first organized community and was established maybe 10,000 years ago. The present village of Cape Denbigh is built on this same site.

My Aunt Kiiriq's ancestral tribesmen lived at this first village and handed down their history to her by word of mouth; she repeated it over and over, until it became a part of her. As she repeated it to me, I wrote it down, and I now pass it on to the reader. One of the stories she told me is this epic legend which follows, in which the main character is an eagle-man.

The eagle-man lived with his parents on the south tip of a peninsula which had a high cliff. Like many characters found in Unaliq legends, this man was capable of turning from human to animal (an eagle, in this case) and vice-versa. When he was transformed into an eagle, he was a great flyer, had the instincts of an eagle, and was able to hunt sea mammals by clawing them. Whenever he returned to his home on the cliff, he transformed himself into a human.

The story begins with life among the surviving members of the eagle-men who lived at the end of the Cape Denbigh peninsula as cliff dwellers. This peninsula, which, according to legend, was once an island, lies between Norton Bay on the western side and the Shaktoolik mountain range on the eastern side. The distance between the island and the mountain range is about eighteen miles. The area of the sea eventually receded, and the lowland that formed there became a bridge between Cape Denbigh Island and the eastern mountain range. Many years were required for this process, and the land was not inhabited until the latter part of an era when super-natural giants and eagle-men lived in this particular area.

Just before the expiration of the first known era of supernatural beings, the first human family migrated to the virgin tundra and settled on the coast of this eighteen-mile stretch of lowland. The legend teller himself did not know who they were or where they came from, but he thought they came from the south. This family had only one child, and she was a young woman. The surviving family of eagle-men was an aged mother and her son. Since the father had died, this only son had become a great hunter. His aged mother, though quite feeble, was able to live a long life with her son.

One evening when he returned home from his flights over the countryside, the eagle-man surprised his mother by bringing back a female human. This female was destined to become a prime factor in the change of supernatural humanity to natural man, and to bring about the move from the cliffs to a new homesite called Ayaatayat.

When the eagle-man moved his family to Ayaatayat, or Nukleet, the first community at Cape Denbigh cove, his supernatural ability ceased to func-tion and he lost his eagle skin and tail. According to the legend, this was a stage of transition, and he lived a life of duality while he built a home on the eastern slope of Cape Denbigh.

The Unaliq legends have peculiar characters, and these people lived a longer span of life. Since Cape Denbigh was an island, the eagle-man did not find a woman for his wife until the land had formed between these two ranges of mountains. The eagle-man had searched for other humanity long before his transformation into a human himself. Every day he flew to far-off countries. Then, one day, when he came back from his adventures, his aged mother encouraged him to try again to search for a wife from the coastal region.

When he left his aerie home of rocky pinnacles, the eagle-man decided to glide low over the tundra. As he was flying, he thought he saw a moving object which ap-peared to be like a human walking on the tundra. He did not wish to startle the lone person, so he landed some distance away, for he did not know the nature of what he had found. As soon as he landed, he took his eagle-skin suit off and turned into a man. He approached the figure, and when he walked nearer he noticed that the being was a woman. Then he advanced very quickly to her. As he came closer he noticed that she was trembling with fear, and so he spoke to her first, "I will not harm you, dear woman; I am a man, not an eagle. Please sit down and tell me all about yourself and where you live."

She managed to smile before she sat down. He sat down also, in front of her; as he did, he smiled at her.

She showed him her little wooden bucket and its contents as she exclaimed, "I picked these salmonberries for my parents, but I want you to eat them . . . you must be hungry."

"Aa, quyaana, yes, thank you," he said.

While he was eating, she told him about her parents, where they lived, and how they came to live at this particular place. "My parents built our igloo, our sod house, near the mouth of the river," she explained and pointed in the direction of the river. "I am the only child. Many times I wish I could have been a man instead of a woman. Then I might have been a good hunter like you."

He did not try to show his sympathy. Instead, he peered beyond her to find the location of her home.

Before they parted, he asked her not to reveal his identity to her parents, for he decided to win her hand by bringing food to them. As he stood up, he designated a special place of landing next time he visited, "When I come back, I will land on the beach below your igloo and approach this landing from the direction of the sea. You must watch for my arrival and search for some seals on the beach."

Before he left he pointed toward Cape Denbigh and said, "I live on that peninsula. I will see you again, soon."

"Piuřarin, goodbye," she said, and she waved farewell.

After he left and disappeared in the sky, she began to pick berries vigorously. In no time, she filled her bucket and left, walking very fast. While she was walking, she remembered not to reveal her secret. But with an unusual experience, how was she to keep a secret? She said to herself, "I'll sew a larger pair of mukluks, presumably for myself, but in reality for my new friend."

Every day she searched for the sign of his coming. One day she saw a huge dead seal on the beach. As she walked nearer to it, she identified the animal. "Ugřuk, bearded seal, our favorite food," she said loudly.

She left it immediately and ran up to the igloo to announce her find to her parents, "I found a fresh ugřuk on the beach and I'm going to butcher it now. We'll have some of it for supper."

She took her ulu, her woman's knife, and ran back to the beach. Her parents followed, since it is customary to butcher large animals together. Her mother was in charge and Kunuřang, the daughter, observed carefully the method of dressing it: first the ugřuk was doused with water; then the flippers and the head were cut off and the belly was split wide open, exposing thick layers of blubber next to the skin; then her mother slashed the blubber off the flesh of the body; she removed the internal organs and laid them aside in a clean wooden pan; and the final procedure of dissecting was done by the father. Some of the meat was hung on the racks, and the blubber was cut in strips for rendering and placed in prepared seal pokes or skin containers. While all this work was in progress, her mother prepared the choicest parts of the ugřuk for their supper, and Kunuřang prepared the meal on a campfire, during which time she quietly subdued her emotions about the secret that soon would be revealed to her parents. This episode was the beginning of her cherished experiences; another one, somewhat like it, would soon follow.

Thereafter, the eagle-man left other varieties of sea mammals for their food. Her parents began to wonder where all these animals had been brought from and by whom.

Then, one day, he comé privately to her. As they sat on a driftwood log, he put his arms around her and kissed her nose and rubbed it gently. They both laughed and embraced happily. He spoke first, "Will you be my wife, Kunuřang, my love?"

She nodded her head and he lifted her up and would have taken her away if she had not suddenly withdrawn and reminded him, "My parents; I cannot leave them now. You haven't seen them yet. Will you come into our igloo to meet them? Perhaps you could ask them if we could get married. Be sure to explain, also, that you are the one who brought fresh seals to us."

He accepted her suggestion and entered the semisubterranean igloo for the first time. As they entered the dark tunnel, he took her in his arms and held her tightly. He said to her, "I'm worried, Kunuřang; they might not let me have you for my wife. Please tell them that I love you and that you love me, too, will you?"

Instead of signifying her affirmative answer, she took his face in her hands and rubbed her nose to his and allowed him to hold her more closely.

She entered through the trap door which was part of the floor by pushing it upward, and at that moment her parents saw a man emerging also, while their daughter was holding the cover of the entrance open. They stood side by side. Then, she introduced her companion to her parents, "Aapaang, Aakaang, uvvaa anguniaqtigřavut, Father, Mother, here is our hunter."

"Ki, go," her father commanded, "and prepare some food for him, and after he has eaten, he can rest."

The young hunter sat down, dispelling his built-up anxiety, and watched Kunuřang as she laid the food before him. He kept thinking, "Will her father accept my proposal?"

Occasionally, he was asked questions about his homeland and family. He ate hurriedly because he wanted to present his proposal to the girl's parents. After he wiped his hands, he moved closer to her parents and asked them if he could marry their daughter.

Before her father answered his question, he turned to his wife for approval. She smiled at him approvingly. His future father-in-law then answered, "It is not customary for one to choose his own wife among us. But since I do not have a group from which to select a husband for my daughter, I will consent to the proposal—however, only under these circumstances: first, my wife and I would like to have you bring her home for an occasional visit while we are living. She is the only child we have. Second, if your child is a girl, my wife and I will raise her so that our generation will not terminate."

His statement of adoption left the young couple pondering. However, they both agreed to his plan, and the eagle-man promised her parents that he would bring her back to see them once every year.

The first marriage in the Denbigh area took place that same evening. The ceremony of marriage was a simple procedure: they merely stood together before the parents and promised to work together all through their lives, to support themselves and any offspring. Then the feast was arranged by the girl's parents. To honor the new member of the family, the bride arranged choice food on a wooden plate and presented it to her husband to eat; his acceptance of the food was an indication that from the day of marriage she was his wife. After the feast, they danced and sang their songs.

The next morning, they all gathered wild edible greens, berries, and roots. They also dried meat and made Eskimo ice cream to take home to his aged mother, since she was not able to attend the wedding ceremony. The eagle-man was very anxious to present his wife to his mother, so they both flew away to his home on the Cape Denbigh bluff.

When they arrived, he landed at the usual place. After his transformation to a man, he led his bride to the rocky cave where his aged mother lived.

"My mother will be pleased to meet you, Kunuřang. Please allow me to go in the igloo first, as she isn't expecting another woman to enter our home."

When he entered, he smiled first then called her, "Aakaang, Mother, I brought you a daughter-in-law. This is my wife, Kunuřang."

He led his wife to his mother and made her sit close to her. She welcomed the bride approvingly.

"Irniaqa, my son, bring the largest spotted seal poke from our cache." Then she sang a wedding song in the ancient Unaliq language:

> "I welcome you to our midst
> Paniing, my daughter
> Enter in...to the bosom of our home
> Enter in...to the life of the Unalit

The yuit, people of Yupik
Piqpagiyumain ilaqautigran, love your husband
To the end of your service."

As the eagle-man entered, he remained still until his mother finished singing the song, the melody which would dwell in his heart.
Then he handed the container to his mother who stretched out her
arms with delight, smiling an unusual smile. She gave a bundle to her
daughter-in-law, "It is for you. Put it on and wear it."

A second one she gave to her son, saying, "Son, for you. Put it on
and wear it tonight."

The wedding festival was celebrated with a feast and dancing and
singing. "The last of its kind," the old mother thought, with a goodbye feeling and a sad heart. Yet, she couldn't suppress a feeling of
happiness in her heart, for she knew it was also the beginning of the
history of prolonging their tribe, the Yuit of the Unalit.

The couple lived for a year as cliff dwellers. Kunuřang was very
happy, and yet a tugging sensation kept creeping in—an urge to visit
her parents. Her child would soon be delivered. Her husband promised her that after the baby was born and purified they would leave for
an extended visit.

"Now that you are heavier, I will have to exert more strength to
carry you over." He smiled.

She smiled with tears welling in her eyes and nodded her head,
"How can I bear to part with my little eagle-baby?" and she collapsed
in her husband's arms.

Both felt the internal agony. He comforted her with a promise that
they would have a chance to love the baby while she was nursing her.

After the customary rites of purification had been performed, the
eagle-man took his family to his wife's home. When they presented
the baby, Kunuřang announced, "She is a little girl. May I nurse her
while I'm here?"

Her father assented to her request and said, "We hope you'll live
with us for the summer."

Kunuřang glanced at her husband at this moment, as he said, "I will have to leave my wife occasionally in order to support and visit my aged mother."

Kunuřang's mother did not realize that the little eagle-girl, now her daughter, would become the first mother at the new settlement called Chaxtuliq, the old word for Shaktoolik. For during those times, before history was written, it was customary for Eskimos to marry their next of kin in order to perpetuate their population and their heritage.

Mr. and Mrs. Eagle-man provided her parents' survival necessities: Kunuřang supplied them with edible greens, roots, and berries, and he with the wild game from land and sea.

Mr. Eagle-man announced one morning to his wife that it was time to depart to their home. Again, the departing from their loved ones was at hand. His father-in-law thanked him for the adoption of the little girl and for the gifts of food and their company.

Thus parted the only known inhabitants of the Cape Denbigh and Shaktoolik wilderness. When the eagle-man's family arrived at their home, Kunuřang presented her mother-in-law with fresh food, now that their old mother was unable to gather it. The eagle-man hunted daily for mammals in the sea and animals on the land. Kunuřang was very busy. Their mother's duty at home was to transfer traditional oral literature to her family, so she would sing songs and recite stories. Kunuřang memorized all she could for the purpose of unfolding the beautiful stories to her future children. It was the duty of parents to teach their children to preserve their life-long experiences and to relive their past in songs, legends, mythology, and folktales.

Kunuřang enjoyed her mother-in-law's renditions. Often she would request to have her repeat the songs and stories. And, on these occasions, her husband would come in and sit down by her side and request that they leave the igloo to plan the vacating of their old home. He did not wish to disturb his mother.

One time he took her up on the ridge of Cape Denbigh and pointed to an area where they might move. "Our cave will soon disintegrate and fall to the depths of the sea. Will you help my mother when she tries to pack her things? I will transport our survival food by flying several flights to the place I've selected."

"Ii-i, yes!" Kunuřang accepted his plan. "How are we to tell our mother?"

"We'll go in right now to announce to her our future plans."

The mother accepted the plan, but in her thoughts she questioned whether she would be able to stand the exposure to the new environment.

For several days he did the hauling while the women cleared the igloo by packing. The day before their departure they retired early. But before she went to sleep, his mother asked her son to come to her. When he came, she handed him a seal poke which was bulging with something for her son.

"The contents are yours. Keep and guard them. They are your father's intricate patterns for tools for making items for your survival. You might need them in the future."

"Thank you, mother," said the eagle-man. "Try to rest tonight and be ready to take a flight with me to our future home tomorrow."

He did not realize, then, what the circumstances the passing of time would bring to him.

He woke up first, and, as it was customary for him to examine the weather, he went out. He went up to the highest pinnacle and sat down, looking skyward, westward, and eastward, and read the peripheral signs of weather for the day.

In the meantime, his wife began preparations for the day. While she was setting the table, she thought of their old mother. Kunuřang dropped the utensils, and went over to her. She touched the mother's shoulders to wake her up, but the older woman did not move nor respond. The daughter-in-law was alarmed but not quite sure and touched her arm again; it was cold and lifeless. Then she realized that her mother-in-law had died during her sleep.

She ran out, but then she slowed her pace and walked calmly up to where her husband was sitting. Before she arrived, he met her. Without announcing to him about her mother-in-law, she sang a death song to her husband using the lyrical words:

"Our mother spirit has left her,
Our mother spirit has also left us.
Come and see, Oh! come and see!"

Kunuřang held his arm comfortingly, and they walked to the igloo inside of the cliff. As they entered the igloo, the death song he had heard made him feel less emotional. He said, "We will not disturb my mother; she looks comfortable there."

Before they left that day, they rolled a stone over the entrance, sealing it safely with other stones.

Now he knew why she had given the precious implements to him before she went to sleep. They paused before the tomb, and stood quietly and repeated their prayer to "Silam Inua," their invisible Owner of the Universe. While they were standing there, a group of ravens flew overhead, crowing and dipping their wings toward them. They interpreted the birds' behavior as a sign of wishing them good luck in their new venture. The ravens were dropping their load of good prospects for hunting seasons ahead of them. This little act of the ravens brought their thoughts of sadness back to reality. He wiped away his tears and said, "I'll take you over to our new place first so that you can build a fire and cook our meal. And in the meantime, I'll haul our things. Is it all right with you?"

"Ii-i!" she replied approvingly. "After lunch, I will build a cache right away and you can build a temporary hut for us. Then we'll have storage and shelter for ourselves and our belongings before it rains."

"I am fortunate to have found you," smiled the eagle-man as he spoke. "From now on you'll take the place of my mother."

She responded with the gesture of leaning against his side.

The flight to the new location took only a few minutes. He helped her get some dry wood first before he flew back to their old home. Each time he returned, he seemed to be more jovial. They completed their tasks as they had planned.

The next day he said to his wife, "We'll rest today and enjoy our new home and surroundings. We'll have to select a name for our new place."

"That's a good suggestion," said his wife. "I'll enjoy exploring this place, looking for many wild edible greens, roots, and berries (since some vegetables do not grow in our old mountain habitat). I am glad our new home faces the east; it will be warmer, too. The sun will rise over the Shaktoolik range of mountains. I can see my parents' home. Below us on the left is a beautiful cove where a river tumbles over the ravine down to Chinggiaq Sound. Right below our place, there is a seashore where we could set our net to catch fish, seal, and beluga. Besides these prospects, there are many small coves where much dirftwood is lodged." Kunuřang chatted like a little squirrel.

"I noticed them as I flew over these low palisades, too," he replied, chiefly to encourage her to continue to talk. He understood her motive and appreciated her companionship. It helped to relieve his grief.

She continued, "You and I can take a walk tomorrow and select the four poles and other types of driftwood which we'll need for building material. I can carry lighter poles and you the heavier ones."

She stopped talking and looked at him wonderingly and said, "Why are you so quiet tonight? Is there anything wrong?"

"No," he said. "But I must tell you about a physical change that has taken place tonight. I . . . I lost my supernatural power as I left my pinnacle; luckily, I managed to land safely, halfway on the ground. There, I dismantled my eagle-skin suit. Now I can no longer fly. Moreover, I left some of our things over there."

She hugged him instead of expressing her thoughts. They clung together, both wondering how they could possibly visit her parents.

Finally, her husband withdrew and said, "Let's rest in our little hut, for I am very tired."

They walked to their temporary home and retired.

Once a supernatural being, this now natural man emerged with his wife into the new era of time to begin the story of historical man; he was the first ancestor of the Unaliq Eskimos.

The Ogre Baby, Makkatahlungiq

Their new homesite at Ayaatayat was protected from the north winds and faced a gentle slope on the eastern side. It was situated above the high walls of the cliff below them, and it was a beautiful place. A nearby brook provided them with fresh water, as it ran to its outlet in the cove.

The high wall of the embankment stretched continuously toward the north and connected itself to the lowlands. Below, their future village would face a sea-blue cove of the Bering Sea, an ideal place to hunt sea mammals such as beluga, fish, and seals. Above them on the higher range grew berries, and all kinds of edible vegetation were plentiful nearby. The beach against the cliff was loaded with a supply of driftwood and crustaceans. The driftwood, a wealth of a natural resource, would provide them with igloo frames to support their underground abodes and frames for their umiaks and kayaks. It would also serve for making wooden utensils, tools, and weapons, as well as firewood to provide them with warmth. The village, now permanently instituted as a close-knit community, had a wise leader, one who was once an eagle-man.

It was customary from the beginning that the greatest hunter of the community should take his place as a chief; from there on, his status was handed down through the generations to his son or to his daughter when he died. The chief, having power to direct and protect his people, was responsible for their safety. The present chief of Ayaatayat

15

did not realize one evening that his own lineage would also become a factor in causing a catastrophe.

When he went to bed, though he was tired, he felt uneasy. He finally fell asleep, but he slept soundly for just a few hours. It must have been about midnight when he was awakened by a queer sound. He turned his face toward the sound and witnessed a strange sight. His grandchild had eaten its mother's right breast and was now eating the left one. He knew what it meant; he must act quickly! He assembled his remaining family at once and assigned them to awaken all the people of the village with a message to tell them to flee for their lives immediately.

Within a short time, the people had dressed and an orphaned young man was chosen to lead them away on a northern route. The chief, stricken with grief, walked behind his people. While they were fleeing, the chief called to the leader to stop and rest for awhile. He said to him that he had forgotten to take his knife (such tools were very valuable to the ancient Eskimo people).

He then offered the young men an opportunity to do a great favor for him, in honor of their chief; he would give them a chance to fulfill his wishes even at the risk of dangerous consequences. He said, "If anyone volunteers to get my knife from the village, and succeeds, I will offer him my chiefhood and in time he will become my son-in-law."

The orphan immediately accepted the challenge. The chief laid his hands in the young man's hand and said, "Silam Inua, the Owner of the Universe, will give you strength and wisdom to escape from the baby ogre."

The young man appeared proud to serve his chief when he answered, "I will recover your knife, your honor."

And he ran toward the deserted village, for he was a swift runner.

Some people said, "He will never come back alive."

They were superstitious and concerned for his safety, but his grandmother quieted them and said, "I have great faith in my grandson. He'll come back safely. Let us continue to travel, the ogre might catch up with us."

The chief took the lead until they reached the last slope of the twelve-mile ridge. He then turned left and walked until he reached a jutting protrusion of land and waited for his people. There he made plans with the older men regarding what their destination should be. He felt sorry, especially for the aged people and the small children, so he said, "We will cross this bay and lodge at the old, old village site (now known as Dexter Point). We can stay overnight there and rest until the young man overtakes us."

They agreed with his plans and started their journey, walking on the ice toward the opposite shore of the bay where there was a little hill called Tachiq.

In the meantime, the young brave was approaching the deserted village, and as he cautiously approached the chief's igloo, he stopped behind a willow so he could spot the baby ogre and have time to plan his action to his best possible advantage. Just as he focused his view toward the next to the last igloo of the village, he saw the baby ogre climbing out of the window. The orphan knew the ogre's next move would be toward the last igloo of the village. He was glad that the wind was blowing from the north, for it was blowing his scent away from the direction of the ogre. Otherwise, the ogre might have smelled him by now.

The baby ogre was a terrible sight. Its mouth had enlarged from ear to ear and was lined with large, sharp teeth, and it had its parka and diapers on. Instead of being afraid, the orphan felt sorry for the baby ogre for he knew that something had happened to decree this terrible metamorphosis. Its mother must have failed to abide by the traditional rituals as she was instructed to do.

When the ogre crawled to the next igloo, it was crying in an unnatural way, which made it feel buoyantly light, and it decided to jump down through the window into the igloo. When the ogre crawled in the last igloo the orphan ran very fast toward the chief's igloo. And as he jumped in and landed on the floor he spotted the knife on its rack. He noticed that the knife was in its sheath and attached to a belt. As he was tying the belt around his waist he dashed out the tunnel and stopped at the entrance and listened. He didn't hear the ogre's cries so he ran up the west path back toward his people. As he climbed up the hill he turned toward the village just in time to see the baby ogre following him; luckily, however, it was just at the foot of the hill above the village. He knew the baby ogre was a monster with power to overtake him, and he would have to run faster to escape it, for he was only a young man without magic.

He ran moderately fast. He remembered his grandmother's advice: "If you wish to escape from danger by running, run at an even pace so you won't get too exhausted."

When he turned around to gauge the distance between him and the enemy, the baby ogre was closer to him. He could hear its cries clearly now, and as it cried the loudest, the breast-shaped little hills would project out on the ridge of the (Nukleet) peninsula.

He was racing for his life, and the pursuer was overtaking him. So in order to detain it, he first dropped his mittens; the second time, his hood; the sleeves one at a time; and, finally, he tore his parka into smaller pieces. Each time he dropped a piece of clothing, he was able to get ahead while the ogre stopped to eat his clothes.

Shortly after he dropped the last piece, he came to the last slope of the twelve-mile ridge, and as he came down to the edge of the coast he saw, on a white expanse of deep snow, the caribou tracks which led toward the Shaktoolik range of mountains beyond. An idea leaped into his mind at this crucial point. He expressed his thoughts loudly, "I shall plunge into the snow and cut off my human scent."

He ran further, this time on the caribou tracks, until he saw a crevice filled with soft snow. Before he plunged in, he looked once more at the ogre to see if it had followed, crawling along the caribou tracks. The ogre was at the spot where the caribou tracks left the mainland where it had stopped to smell around to find the orphan's tracks. When it started over the caribou tracks toward him, he plunged into the spot about ten feet away from the tracks and covered himself with snow.

He held his breath very lightly so the ogre would not hear him breathe. He listened. The ogre's crying and the sounds of its crawling became louder and louder as it crawled closer and closer. The young man covered his mouth with the palms of his hands and waited to be attacked.

When the ogre's crawling sounds came from further and further away, the orphan thanked the supernatural power who was able to give him wisdom to escape his pursuer, the dangerous baby ogre.

He knew he was safe when he could no longer hear the baby ogre's cries. Instead of walking on the caribou tracks, he walked on the soft snow and made his way back to the mainland. He found his group's tracks to the old village site.

When he approached the group, he was met by his grandmother, then by the chief, and last by his beautiful future wife. The chief warned the people not to talk loudly out-of-doors. They were all very uncomfortable and tired when he arrived.

The chief said to them, "We will move to the lowlands and build our village on the edge of the Taguumaniq River. There we will celebrate to thank Silam Inua for our safety and to the young man who has proven his bravery. We will stay here for a while, at least for a day longer, and we shall go back to our old village only to get our belongings, such as tools, food, and our dogs and sleds. From now on we will not hunt the caribou anymore, for I am sure you will hear the baby ogre crying amidst the herd."

From the time of that catastrophe at Ayaatayat, the old village, until the Gospel came and was preached, the Eskimo hunters would hear the baby crying in the caribou herd. And when the Gospel came, the crying ceased forever.

The Battle Song of the Giants

Many thousands of years ago, giants, cannibals, and strange animals lived in the wilderness of Alaska. The Eskimos tell about them in their legends, myths, folktales, and special songs. The roaming Eskimos called Nunamiut tell epic stories to their children; and, when the children become parents, they tell the same stories to their children. So, these stories which people relate are not forgotten because the stories are interesting and are somewhat like the round songs with no end. This story was handed to me, so it is my duty to hand it down to you. The Eskimo children listen attentively and learn to tell stories themselves.

One time in the wilderness, some Inupiaq Eskimos lived in a temporary village. Their village was built on a riverbank. Their leader, a chief, had one son, and the chief and his wife loved him very much. So the chief made a rule that no one should leave the village alone; the hunters must hunt together in a group. Why? Because the village leader's duty is to protect his subjects. But sometimes the people don't always obey the rules of their towns, so they get into trouble, get lost, or even lose their lives.

One day, the chief's son and two companions left their village to hunt for caribou, and they did not come home for a long time. Their parents and other villagers were worried about them, fearing that they may have been kidnapped by the giants. The chief sought daring volunteers to search for the three young hunters, but no one dared to leave town.

In the same village there was an orphan named Inuuřaq. This young man was the only one who decided to search the wilderness for the missing hunters. Since the orphan had no kayak or weapons, he asked his grandmother to do an errand for him: "Nengzurluung, dear Grandma, do you think the chief would let me use his kayak and weapons? Will you ask him if I may use them? Tell him I'll search for the lost hunters."

"Do you think he'll let you go alone?" his grandmother asked.

"He might, because his son may be living yet," Inuuřaq answered hopefully.

"You're a brave man," she said and left.

When she entered the leader's igloo, the chief and his wife were sitting on the floor, both wearing a worried look. The chief's wife directed her to sit down before them.

The chief spoke first, "Has anyone heard any news about the three young hunters?"

"No, Chief, but I come on an errand for Inuuřaq, my grandchild, to ask if he may use your kayak and weapons as he is searching for the hunters."

"Ah! Ahmiyuah! Yes, that is good news. My equipment is handy; tell him my wife will help him to take the kayak down to the river." The chief managed to smile as he spoke. He got up, raised his arms toward the ceiling window, and asked Silam Inua, our God, to give Inuuřaq strength and courage on his way to the wilderness. "You tell Inuuřaq not to leave this evening. It is too late now and the giants will get him."

"Ah, Ataniq, yes, Chief." She thanked him as she left the igloo.

Inuuřaq met her in their yard. She said to him, "You may leave early tomorrow morning."

"But, I'll get ready now, Grandma, and please gather my travelling clothes and put them in my sack. Be sure to include my sword-knife; I might need it out there."

Inuuřaq went to the chief's house to prepare the load he would carry in his kayak. The chief's orderly helped him to carry the kayak over to his yard.

Early the next day, Inuuřaq left. As he paddled through the serpentine river, Inuuřaq practiced maneuvering with his double-bladed paddle. He practiced his marksmanship by shooting drifting wood with his bow and arrow as the logs passed swiftly by. Since he travelled day and night, he got very tired. Late one evening he dragged his kayak to the riverbank, turned his kayak over, and crawled inside the hollow space to sleep through the night.

He travelled for many days until he reached the high plateau region. When he came to the crests of the hills, Inuuřaq would crawl on his hands and knees instead of walking so none of his enemies would see him. On one particular evening while searching for his friends, he saw a shiny, round animal on the sandbar. He crawled back to his kayak and planned his strategy. Since the huge animal was asleep, he might be able to get very close to it. He started his attack by crawling through the grass. When he came nearer, he identified it as a giant shrew, ugřungnaqpak. Rather than being afraid of it, he recalled a story that his grandmother had once related of how a brave man killed a shrew. He decided to fling his arrow to the place where the neck met the backbone. Inuuřaq stood up and flung his arrow, and as it lodged in the shrew's neck the animal stood up to face the boy. He ran to the animal and plunged his sword-knife into its heart. When it fell, he thought to himself, "It will never kill people anymore."

To make sure that it was dead, Inuuřaq cut off its head and thought, "I'll take this with me and give it to the chief if I get home safely."

He tied the shrew's head on a spruce tree which was located near the river. Then he left the remains on the higher land of the sandbar and covered them with rubble so that other animals would not scatter its parts.

When he resumed his journey, the shallows of a ford hindered his progress and made him tired. So, when he came to a hillside cove on the edge of the river, he made his camp and rested again.

The next day as he paddled around the last river bend, he saw a large giants' igloo and a smaller one. He pulled his kayak up the bank to rest and to plan the procedure which might lead him to a successful skirmish with the giants. When he finished, he put his sheath with his sword-knife around his waist, and, instead of paddling his kayak, he decided to walk over to the igloos as quietly as he could, like a spy.

Before he entered one igloo, he gripped his weapon securely in his palm, then he lifted the skin flap on the door. He stood face to face with the first giant and his giant wife. He thought of the epic stories that he had heard when he was a little boy.

"Ya!, awe, how did you manage to escape from the giant shrew, little man?" the giant roared.

Inuuřaq had no time to answer the giant's question because at this moment the giant leaped to a wall opposite from the entrance of the igloo where Inuuřaq was standing. The giant took a big ulu by its handle and held it forward at his arm's length and began to draw it forward and backward as he sang the battle song:

> "U-va-nii! U-va-nii! U-va-nii!
> Right here! Right here! Right here!
> Heya, hey-ya hey!
> I'll fling my ulu at you!"

Inuuřaq shifted his position to one side and the ulu lodged on the wooden wall with a twang. Inuuřaq dislodged the ulu and repeated the giant's tactics of maneuvering the weapon back and forth, singing the giant's song, but instead of "U-va-nii, right here," he sang:

> "Ki-va-nii! Ki-va-nii! Ki-va-nii!
> In there! In there! In there!
> Heya, hey-ya hey!
> I'll fling my ulu at you!"

As he flung the ulu, he heard the alarming cry "Iiřigii!" by the giant's wife when her husband's severed head rolled over and lodged by her side. She said, "You little imp, I'll punish you, too."

When she took the ulu from the wall, Inuuřaq said, "You will die also unless you show me where your captives are."

Disregarding the offer, and singing the battle song, she aimed her ulu at her enemy but missed, and again Inuuřaq was too swift. Her head rolled over and lodged by her husband's head.

Inuuřaq carried the giant ulu out of the death igloo and laid it on a stump. As he was walking towards the smaller igloo he said to himself, "The chief will be amused by and marvel at such a huge ulu."

He entered the igloo and found the three starving hunters who had been bound tightly to the poles and rafters of the igloo. As Inuuřaq cut off their fetters, the prisoners fell helplessly on the floor and cried, showing their relief. They were saved from starvation.

Inuuřaq fed them and took care of them until they were able to walk to his kayak. He placed two men inside his kayak, one in the front part and the other in the back part. Then the chief's son sat in the cockpit with him. Inuuřaq said to his companions, "Mummak, chief's son, and I will exchange places with you when we get tired of steering our kayak. O yes! I must get the ulu! It will be given to our chief, and the ugřungnaqpak's head also. Mummak, you remind me to stop at the place where I killed the animal. I believe it is at the tenth river bend from here."

"Ah, yes," answered his curious kayak mate. "I'm anxious to see the shrew's head."

As they neared the village, they heard the people's welcome yelling and laughing. When the four men arrived they were led to the qařgi.

Inuuřaq became a highly honored hero. During the celebration that particular night, he presented his gifts to his chief. And, thereafter, the hunters and food gatherers sought their food without fear from the giants.

Imitchaq's Hero

The Imitchaq people located their permanent village site on a cliff. One explanation for the choice was that the location offered protection from the ocean flood, wild animals, or possibly from attacks by their enemies, the Indians.

On the coast near Imitchaq lies a peninsula where people once went around its terminal tip without being molested. They went in their large skin boats and smaller kayaks, and even afoot along the shore. During this time many years ago, there appeared a strange, large flat octopus. It was a strange sea animal shaped somewhat like a stretched walrus skin. It had many studded arms, like an octopus, on its outer skin. These contained suckers which it used to crush boats or people as they skirted around the jetty in their umiaks and kayaks.

The population decreased more and more every summer. Furthermore, this situation made the inhabitants fearful as well as hungry. There appeared not a single brave man to annihilate the monster. Rather, the people began to take shortcuts over the neck of the peninsula. The travellers would haul their boats and things over the peninsula instead of sailing around it as they formerly had done.

It was in such an environment that Ilaganiq and his brothers were reared at Imitchaq village. Consequently, their father and mother instilled in their sons' minds a plan as to how they might kill the enemy. So they encouraged their sons to exercise physically and to practice their bow and arrow skills to prepare them for the coming ordeal.

Ilaganiq, who had webbed hands and feet, had become the fastest runner, swimmer, a sharp-shooter, and the most skillful hunter, so he was chosen to kill the Amikuk, the skin octopus. By now, Ilaganiq had acquired a powerful physique. So he accepted the challenge by addressing his aged father: "Aapaang, I will kill it with my two knives. I'll maneuver my kayak onto the water over it. Then I'll sit like a decoy and let it attack me. When I see its tentacles protruding out of the water, I'll dive into the body of the skin octopus and begin immediately to tear it apart once I am folded into its bosom."

He smiled as he showed his father how he would swing right and left to kill it. His father became so excited that he got up and waved his arms right and left with his son. He said, "Ilaganiq, come with me to the cliff."

Ilaganiq followed his father.

When they arrived at the high place, his father lifted his hand up to the sky and prayed to Silam Inua, their God whom they called the Owner of the Universe and whom the Eskimos often asked to help them in times of stress and trouble. He is also called the Great Spirit whom one cannot see but can feel his strength and guidance.

Ilaganiq said to his parents, "You can watch me while I am performing the feat."

He told his father before he left them, "Tonight I will sharpen my knives and place them on my wrist band."

The family retired early, and no one else was aware of the coming event which would make him the greatest hero.

The next day, early, the whole family watched. His brothers went with him to the peninsula, and as they crawled on their stomachs their brother Ilaganiq warned, "No talking!"

He got into his kayak and paddled toward the jetty. And, as he was ready, he plunged right into the enemy's grip. The boys saw the battle as Ilaganiq tore the octopus apart. The evidence of killing, red blood and bits of animal flesh, floated on the surface of the troubled sea.

All this happened very quickly, but several times Ilaganiq surfaced for air after he freed himself from the dying monster. He then cut the babiche rope from his side, and tied it firmly to the animal before he surfaced the third time. He pulled his kayak to him, entered it, and paddled ashore to the jetty. There he pulled himself out of the kayak and pulled the dismembered corpse onto the beach. As he stood over the beast exposed on the rocks he said, "Here lies the enemy of my people at Imitchaq and others who live on the coast of the Bering Sea. Now they can travel and live without fear."

The Creation of the
First Festival

The creation of the festivals has a mythical origin which began back in the days of the eagle-man as told in the first legend. According to the story, a mother eagle wanted to originate a festival which would bring pleasurable music to the inhabitants of the dark, primeval world. She and her son were the last mythical eagle-people who lived on the pinnacle of a high mountain. Although they were like eagles, they had power to transform themselves into human beings.

O ne day an eagle-woman sent her son out on a flying trip to search for a human being who would be willing to learn to sing songs to accompany dancing and folktales. If he found a man, he was to capture him and bring him to their home. If the man were not willing to come, the son was ordered to kill him.

Soon a man was found. The eagle-man landed nearby, uncovered his head and smiled at his prey. "Don't be afraid of me. See, I am a man like you. Let's sit down so we can talk."

He presented his mother's plan to him. "We will teach you festival songs, dancing, and how to build a qařgi (council house) and how to make a drum."

Trembling, the captive pleaded, "I will go with you . . . but . . . please don't kill me. I am the only living son of my elderly parents whom I am supporting."

"You will not be harmed, I promise. If we are successful with our work, you will be the human originator of festival music."

The captive smiled and nodded his head.

After the captive had been securely fastened onto the eagle-man's back, the two departed to the eagle-man's pinnacle home. As they were circling over his home, the eagle-man said, "Listen!"

"What is that sound?" the captive asked.

"That drumming sound is my mother eagle's heartbeat. We will dance according to its rhythmic thump-thump beating."

At this moment, as they landed on the ridge near their home on the rocky pinnacle, all the captive's feelings of anxiety disappeared. His captor led him into a rock-hewn cave. There the wise mother eagle, sitting on a straw-covered ledge, welcomed them and immediately presented them with the choicest food he had ever tasted.

The training of the human began.

"Tomorrow, I want you, son, and your guest to make the drum. But first, while I am tanning the covering of the baleen whale's liver, bring three saplings. The length will be two wing's stretches long and the thickness will be three fingers' span. You will whittle the top ridge about one middle finger width. This groove will hold the babiche twine when you tie the skin onto the wood framing the drum. Now leave and do, and bring the material."

The wooden frame is made of driftwood which was originally a larch tree. The craftsman usually whittles it down to a desired length and width. He then carves a groove within one-half inch to one inch directly beneath the top rim of the frame. Babiche twine will hold the edges of liver skin in this indentation. Wet twine is wrapped around the circular frame over and over again until the twine is very taut. The drum is then placed in a cool room to dry.

The drum beater is also made from larch tree driftwood. It is about six inches longer than it is wide. It is tapered, with a handle that is thick enough to be easy to hold on to.

This flat drum is beaten on the back side rather than on its face.

This was the beginning of the training of the human. For many days, the eagle-mother and her son taught him how to compose songs and dances, how to beat the drum, and how to organize a festival program.

After the musical repertoire had been received and tested, the pattern for making a council house (qaỷgi) was drafted on a bleached sealskin. Then the preparations for the reunion with his people was excitedly reviewed for the human, since his experience was an extraordinary event.

The greatest event for his people would take place shortly after his arrival. His agenda was prepared something like this: a reunion feast in the qaỷgi; the news about his encounter with the mother eagle and her son; the art of making a drum; the compositions, dances of two types, social and interpretive; how to organize the first sauyak (festival); and how a festival should be introduced to the neighboring communities.

After he returned to his village, the first teacher of the festive celebration announced to his people: "This spring we will invite our neighbors to attend the first celebration of the year. The women will make new parkas and boots, the men will hunt for ugỷuk and other land animals. And we will enlarge our old qaỷgi."

Thus was instituted a new musical program for his people. And ever since that historical beginning, the eagles were considered by the Inupiat, the real people, as the wise originators of the festivals of the Eskimo people of the northern lands.

Mythical Rolling Fire

How did Eskimos teach their children to acknowledge the family customs: morals, obedience and the concept of right and wrong? What criteria did they use to impress upon the children's minds which rules to follow in different situations or problems?

Since the communities did not have established schools, the parents of each family felt responsible for their children's behavior. Folktales, legends and myths were told orally, as stories which have object lessons. These portray misbehavior, kindness, heroic characterizations, or bravery by use of drama, festivals, and dances.

Sometimes the children observed others' performances and listened to the elders. Each story was composed by using something that would depict an example of a character's disobedience and its resulting consequences, or by using examples of good or bad behavior presented to the children as it was narrated to them. The grandparents and elders were the story tellers, either in their homes or in the qaȓgi.

This particular legend, "Mythical Rolling Fire," is a story of undisciplined children. It was originated by the Unaliq tribe. The setting is supposedly at the mouth of Shaktoolik River on the Bering Sea coast about six miles east of Cape Denbigh. Moreover, this episode happened during the spring after the breakup of the river and the sea. At this time, tides and currents bring ice floes from the sea into the river.

There lived in a village a homeless waif who was hired by the chief as a caretaker of the qar̆gi. His name was Iluperaq. Although he was a respected teenager, the ruffians of the same age made his life miserable, especially at night. In order to escape from them, he built his bedroom on the rafters of the council house.

Whenever he heard them coming, he would climb up to his perch. They would call him names, scoff and make fun of his home. After they sang and danced around, some would go home and others would climb on the roof and pound on it.

Late one evening these same ruffians gagged an orphan girl and brought her by force to the edge of the swollen river. They tied her to a heavy log, placed her on an ice floe and pushed her out to the current. One of the spectators was Iluperaq who, when he heard someone crying, went down to see who it was. When he attempted to rescue the girl, the ruffians forcibly tied him to a post. Then they laughed at him, too.

Although her mouth was covered, the helpless girl cried to him for help, urging Iluperaq to get her grandmother. She did not know he was also tied up. While she was drifting, the crying sounds turned to a song:

> "Iluperaq, ikayurkuk
> Iluperaq, help me
> Iluperaq, aqvaung aanaka
> Get my grandmother
> Patagmek, Iluperaq
> Quickly
> Kii...Kii...Iluperaq!
> Please! Please!"

The ruffians laughed at her pleading while they were following the floating iceberg as far as the outlet of the delta. They were like vicious wolves which, after the kill, lick their chops with satisfaction at being so crafty.

They went back to the qar̆gi, leaving the girl on the ice floe and Iluperaq tied to the post. While the boys were in the council house,

Iluperaq broke his bonds and returned there too. It was too late to get help for the girl; the north wind and tide had already taken their victim way out to sea. He felt very sad as he thought of the disobedient who were still clamoring to do some more injustice to the witness of their crime.

While they were dancing around the fireplace, Iluperaq came in to the qaȓgi and climbed through the window onto the roof to look for the unfortunate victim out on the sea, to see if he could rescue her. She was not visible at that moment, because she had turned herself into a rolling fire and was coming with all haste toward the qaȓgi! He ran down the roof, went in and warned the boys, but to no avail. They only laughed at him. So he climbed up to his perch to escape from the approaching rolling fire.

Just after his move, in came the rolling fire with crackling and hissing sounds of "s-s-s-s." It leaped upon the disobedient teenagers and devoured them all. There was not even a mitten left unburned.

Iluperaq cringed at the sight of the catastrophe and felt very helpless.

And so, this is a story about a group of boys who refused to accept the concepts of what is right and what is wrong, and respectful behavior and the consequences of disrespect.

Legend of the Aurora Borealis

The Inupiaq Eskimos call the aurora borealis "kiguruyat" (spirits who gnaw with their teeth). These hissing spirits of the sky, according to Eskimo interpretation, play a football game. The participants wear colorful costumes of many hues. The hissing spirits have the power to entice and hypnotize those who watch their games to the point where they purposely draw their viewers upward into their midst.

Legends, as well as many folktales, were composed primarily as media for teaching moral philosophy. This oral literature was also used to teach discipline, and for recreational purposes and to teach people how to cope with problems endangering their health and survival. This particular legend is an example. It tells a story that could be applied to any disobedient children.

L ate one evening, a boy invited his younger brother to watch the kiguruyat play football. He led his brother farther away from their igloo and they both sat down in the shadow of a willow. "You must not whistle or talk loudly, Tusuk. If you do, they'll come down to us very quickly and they might lift us upward," he warned his brother.

"OK, now tell me the story," Tusuk answered impatiently.

This is the story he told:

One wintry night, many years ago, while two boys were playing outdoors late at night, they heard hissing sounds above their heads. Suddenly they saw a flash of many colors which blinded their eyes.

Kiguruyat approached them unexpectedly. The older brother felt responsible for the safety of his brother so he gave him hurried directions, "Cover your face with your hood quickly! Now, lie flat on the snow like this."

He showed him how by pressing his hooded face against the soft snow, and the boys huddled side by side until the kiguruyat's assault had vanished. They sat up very slowly and crawled to a nearby willow which had been covered partially by a snowdrift. They noticed then that the kiguruyat had moved further away in the sky. The younger brother asked, "What kind of ball are they kicking around up there? And why doesn't it fall to the ground?"

"They are using a child's head, the head of a once disobedient boy who had wandered off, possibly to watch the kiguruyat play football. The reason the ball doesn't fall down to us is because the spirits have powerful magic streets they walk on. The last wanderer was so attracted by the beautiful colors that he forgot to go home."

"And what happened to him?" asked his brother.

"The leaders of the team may have directed one of his men to grab the onlooker. The spirit came down noiselessly, bit the boy's hood, and lifted him bodily by his teeth and brought him up to his group."

"Poor boy, did he cry?" the younger brother asked.

"No! He did not have time to cry because the leader of the team chewed his head off with his sharp fangs. And you know as well as I do, a boy's neck is as frail as this twig," he said at the same moment he broke a twig in two.

"Do you think the kiguruyat are using his head for a football?"

"Yes," answered Qweexoxok.

"We should go home now, Qweexoxok, before they snatch us away, too," suggested his younger brother with fear.

"Let's wait until the kiguruyat run farther away. Here, hold my hand tightly." His brother extended his right hand and gave his final directions, "Hang on to my hand while we run for safety."

Both watched for a chance to escape.

"Now! Run! Cover your mouth and breathe into your parka under your chin."

Just as they reached the skin-covered umiak which was turned upside down on tripods, the kiguruyat came flying overhead. Fortunately the boys hid under the overturned boat.

They squatted down, huddled together. After the hissing sounds had subsided somewhat, the boys ran as fast as they could to their igloo entrance to escape from another attack of the kiguruyat.

"Qweexoxok, if you were not with me the kiguruyat would have taken me away. I will protect my baby brother from now on. I am glad I have a big brother to take care of me."

The moral of the story is: If you can't get a small boy to obey, his older brother or a parent may scare the disobedience out of him.

Wiilingiataq, a Girl Who Refuses to Marry

On the coast of Bering Sound near the outlet of the river once lived two Eskimo families. Wiilingiataq and her family lived on the north bank of Taguumaniq River. And on the opposite bank of the same river lived Chulung and his grandparents. Chulung was already a full-grown man.

In a roundabout way Chulung heard rumors about the pretty girl across the river and that she would not marry any suitor. Her given name paralleled her personality as it meant a girl who refused to marry.

Chulung's curiosity naturally was aroused, until he went every day to sit beneath the riverbank to watch for her. He had pictured her as a beautiful girl with dark, long hair and long, curved black eyebrows and lashes.

He would whisper, "She must be a beautiful girl and I hope she'll soon come out so I can see her closely."

One day she did come out, and she walked very gracefully as she got some water for her parents. At that instant the young man's eyes appeared to stretch and stretch across the whole width of the river until he could see her, seemingly face to face, as she dipped her bucket to draw some water. Then as she turned to go back, his eyes snapped back into their sockets. He felt satisfied to have seen the unconquerable woman.

While he was walking back to his igloo, he planned how he might commence his courtship. Then he thought of an idea: "First, I shall

43

ask my grandfather to help me make a boat out of a large cottonwood log; second, after the boat is finished, I will rub my whole body with caribou tallow (Eskimo perfume) before I call on her."

He entered the igloo and sat down near his grandfather and immediately began to present his plans. He pleaded, "Grandfather, will you help me make a wooden boat? I need a boat that I can use for caribou hunting. The caribou are now visible across the river on the plains."

"If you can bring a large log here, you and I can chisel the pulp out, and we can make a boat for you," his ataata (grandfather) suggested.

"Tomorrow morning, I will haul the log from the beach so that we can start early," planned Chulung enthusiastically.

"It is almost time for us to go to bed," his grandfather replied.

When they sat down to eat, Chulung gobbled his food and his ataata looked at him disgustedly.

"Some strange things will possibly happen to you, Chulung. You are not conforming to the normal ways of eating," his ataata warned him.

All the next day, he tried not to show his excitement in anticipation of the day when he would finally cross the river with his new boat. At the end of the day, the hollowed log had become a real boat. The boat was completely equipped with paddles and an anchor with a line. He and his grandfather launched it.

Chulung invited his grandmother to watch him while he was paddling around on the river. He was now equipped with the boat that he could use to fulfill his plans of courting the lady who lived across the river.

Before they retired for the night, he announced his plans for the next day, "I will leave early tomorrow morning. Do not worry about me, for I am a man now and I can protect myself."

"Ii-i, yes," his grandmother answered with a smile.

Very early the next morning he rubbed himself with caribou tallow, because most women prized the aroma of caribou fat, since only the great hunters were able to kill caribou. This would be a way to entice Wiilingiataq to be his wife.

Feeling very proud, the hopeful suitor crossed the river. After he tied the anchor line to a willow, he climbed over the bank, stepping very carefully and lightly. Then he stopped to examine the igloo. He walked very upright, strutting like a male ptarmigan spreading its beautiful plume before its future bride, as he approached the entrance of the igloo. He opened wide the skin covering of the door and stood before it. A strong breeze blew the caribou aroma into the igloo tunnel. He imagined, "She should smell the aroma by now and possibly come out."

Within a short time he heard her little footsteps. His heart began to thump so loudly that he trembled. "Soon, I should have the chance of proposing to Wiilingiataq."

She came directly to him with her arms stretched out to feel along the tunnel before her, sniffing around him very closely. He was speechless, but he did have sense enough to take her hand and hold it. Finally he heard her speak, "Wait for me for awhile. I'll get my ulu."

When she went back into the igloo for her knife, he ran down to the river to his boat because he did not quite understand her intentions. Did she mean to go for her ulu to kill him or, perhaps, just to slice off a piece of caribou tallow? As soon as he reached his boat, he paddled swiftly away to save his life.

He felt relieved as he reached the opposite shore, for she may have intended to kill him with her ulu. After he had tied the anchor line, he sat down in the early morning shadows of a steep bank overhead.

He watched.

When she came out of the igloo she kept on sniffing, trying to detect the essence of caribou tallow. Like a wild animal she tracked his footprints until she came to the edge of the river. She stood on the shoreline, searching for him; she even walked over to the place where his boat had been tied to the willow sprig.

Chulung felt bad and began to feel sorry for her, but it was too late.

Soon, Wiilingiataq began to sink in the soft mud. She did not make an attempt to move away. Instead, she began to sing a very sad song. To him it sounded like a funeral song about herself:

"Aakaang, nuk ku chaktoing gah
My mother pull me up, come!

> Aapaang, nuk ku chaktoing gah
> My father pull me up, come!
> Nunam eel lqah tug gong qoh
> The earth is swallowing me.
> Qarrain, qilamik
> Come, quickly."

It was a pitiful sight to Chulung. He felt that he should go across and rescue her, but it was too late to act. She was now half submerged in the mire. He wondered why her parents did not heed her calls. Since their door was open, he could hear them quarreling. The mother said, "She is your daughter, my husband."

But the father only said, "She is your daughter, too; you be the first one to pull her out."

Then silence entered their igloo until it became unbearable for both of them. When they finally came out to find their daughter, she had disappeared. She was swallowed up by the earth.

The story portrays an example of the stubbornness of the parents of an Eskimo woman who had refused to conform to the mores of their own culture.

The Legend of Egg Island and Besboro Island

All little children of the world are inquisitive and must be provided with answers to their many questions. The Eskimo storytellers composed unique legends about the geography of their great land.

The Unaliq Eskimos were the original inhabitants of the Norton Sound coast. And there are two islands—one situated near St. Michael and the larger island located fifteen miles out in Norton Sound, opposite the Eskimo villages of Unalakleet, Egavik, and Shaktoolik. Perhaps one curious little Eskimo boy asked about the origin of the two islands while he and his family were out sailing in Norton Sound, "Who put that mountain out in the ocean, grandma?"

Once, long ago, a big giant was travelling on the beach toward the west. He was in a hurry to get back to his home in Siberia. As he was walking on the beach he came to the wall of a big, tall peninsula. Because it was in his way, he took his very large ulu and cut the peninsula off from the mainland. But he did not know what to do with it. He said, "I will braid some basket grass together to make a strong rope."

When he finished, he chiseled grooves on either end of the severed peninsula. Then he tied the rope to it so he could pack it out of the way. He had a very hard time putting the peninsula on his back. When he finally did it, with a big, giant smile he said, "I am the strongest giant of this land."

He started wading out to the deep sea. All of a sudden, his pack fell "kaplunk," splashing water all over him. One of his feet got wet so he sat on this piece of land (which had fallen from his back), took his boot off and took out his insole and replaced it with dry grass he had picked from the land.

"What shall I do with my insole?" he pondered as he examined it. "Oh well, if I leave it here it may become another island, so I'll throw it away as far as I can."

He stood up on the ridge of his new island creation, spat right in the middle of his grass insole, and threw it toward the coast near St. Michael. The grass insole landed on the sea and immediately transformed into another little island and his sputum became a lake. Later, as the ages passed, vegetation grew and many of the rock upheavals became birds' nesting places. Today, the place is called Egg Island.

And the former mainland peninsula of the Shaktoolik range of mountains became the beautiful home of the spotted seals, and it is called by the Eskimos, Qikiqtaq, meaning "island," which the Russians called Besboro Island and that is the name we now use.

Akkamii, the end.

The little boy smiled with satisfaction and thereafter fell asleep. Possibly he dreamed of a big, giant geographer.

Legend of Tree Moss

When you have been walking in the woods, have you ever noticed the moss that hangs from the branches of certain trees? This legend, or old story, tells how the Eskimos believe the moss got on the trees. The story is told to Eskimo children by their parents in order to teach them something very important. Can you find out what this lesson is?

Once upon a time there were two happy old Eskimo ladies. Every spring they travelled from their winter village to a pleasant spot near the seashore to fish in order to have food for the cold, dark, long winter months. Here there were pretty trees, so it was easy for them to pitch their tent. They used branches to cover the dirt floor of their summer home. The fragrance of the spruce made their tent very pleasant. The two old ladies had many things to do here in their fish camp. Besides fishing, they would hunt for duck eggs in the marsh; they would weave birch baskets and make new bowls and spoons from birch wood. They were the busiest old ladies you have ever seen. Can't you hear them laugh and talk while they worked?

Early one morning as they walked along the beach picking up driftwood for their fire, what do you think they saw? They saw many fish jumping, leaping out of the water. It was time to fish. They hurried to their camp to get their net. They cast the net far out into the water and pulled it in full of fish. They did this many times. Soon they were so tired and hungry they had to stop and rest. But they still had much work to do before the day was ended. They had to clean the fish, cut them into strips, and hang them on racks to dry in the sun. This is how the meat was preserved for winter. They saved the choicest parts of several of the fish for dinner.

They built a fire and soon the fish were ready to eat. Then something unpleasant happened. Can you guess what it was? The two old ladies had divided the fish evenly, but there was one piece left over. Both were so hungry that they each wanted it; so they quarreled over a little strip of fish. They slapped and pulled at each other. They even pulled each other's hair so hard that some of it came out and fell on the ground. All of a sudden they heard a strange noise. It seemed to be getting louder and closer. The old ladies were so frightened that they stopped fighting.

"Hurry, let us pack our things and get away from this place," said the first old lady. "If it is the forest giant with his big ulu, he will cut off our heads!"

The two old ladies hurriedly packed their belongings and carried everything to the beach as fast as they could. They even rolled up their path and took it with them so the giant wouldn't be able to find them. As they were loading their belongings into their boat, one old lady suddenly leaned over the side of the boat and listened carefully. What do you think she saw and heard? There in the water was a tiny little needlefish with his mouth wide open singing just as loudly as he could.

That had been the noise which had frightened the old ladies into leaving their fish camp.

The little old lady quickly reached down into the water and snatched up the needlefish, "Well, you little noisemaker! I suppose you think you are pretty smart to cause all this excitement and trouble."

"You were the ones who caused all the trouble by fighting over a little piece of fish. You should be ashamed of yourselves!" replied the needlefish.

The little old lady became angry and said, "Well, we will fix you!"

She took her knife, cut the needlefish in half, and gave one part to her companion. The both gobbled up Mr. Needlefish so he couldn't scold them anymore. Then they sat down and rested. They had had enough excitement for one day. Soon they took everything back to their camping place and set up their tent again. They decided to live peacefully together and not quarrel anymore.

When the little old ladies reached the place where they had first set up their camp, they saw their tangled hair on the ground, and were ashamed. In fact, they were so ashamed that they picked up the hair and threw it as far as they could into the forest. Ever since that time, their hair has been clinging there as tree moss.

What lesson did you learn from this story? Perhaps you would like to sing the song that the needlefish sang when he scolded the two old ladies for being greedy and selfish.

> *Hy-ya-ya! Hy-ya, Hy-ya-ya-ya Hy-ya!*
> *Shame on you! Shame on you!*
> *Both of you! Both of you!*
> *Hy-ya-ya! Hy-ya-ya! Hy-ya!*

How the Orphan Boy Destroys an Eskimo Village

This is a legend of the Unaliq Eskimos who lived at Shaktoolik on the Norton Sound coast four miles east of the present town. It is the story about an orphan who destroyed the village, possibly by supernatural powers. At his command, it turned upside down. The ceiling, the former floor, is still visible today. There are over one hundred circular impressions where igloos once stood. Even those artifacts that in later years were dug from the debris seem to be lying in upside down positions.

There is a moral implication in the story which shows that people are supposed to share with the aged, poor, handicapped, and widows and orphans. In this case the apportioner failed to hand out the meat of the ugřuk, or bearded seal, to the needy. This is the legend as told by the Native storyteller who would take his seat on the woven grass mat in the qařgi in front of his audience at a typical Eskimo gathering.

Once long ago, there lived an orphan boy and his grandmother at the old Shaktoolik village site. The igloo was located at the eastern end of the village. While the children, including the orphan boy, were playing during the late afternoon, the hunters arrived with their sleds heavy with ugřuk. The children were so happy and excited, and they helped to unload the catch into the storerooms. Some ran to their homes to tell the good news, and the orphan went home to tell his grandmother.

As he came in, he called his grandmother, "Nengzuung, we'll have some fresh ugȓuk meat for supper tonight. The hunters brought lots of meat and blubber. Do you think they'll give us some of it?"

"Ii-i, yes. After a little while you can bring your pointed stick carrier for fresh meat to the hunter's igloo to get some for us. The apportioner will give you our share as you present your stick to her. She will pierce the chunks of meat and blubber right through with the stick. You must not drop the meat on the ground as you hurry homeward, since it will be heavy," explained Nengzurluung (dear grandma).

"Aang, yes, Nengzuung," the orphan replied to his grandmother with a smile of anticipation.

The orphan took the sharp-pointed stick carrier and walked out of their igloo and over to the hunter's igloo.

It was customary for children to stand aside by the door until the owner invited them to sit down or asked them if they had come for an errand. As the boy stood there, he watched the butcher and waited for an invitation to extend his stick carrier to her. No one acknowledged his entrance. He stood and stood. Finally, he thought, "Maybe there's no more meat for us."

So he went away without the much-needed food for his grandmother. As he walked back to his igloo he tried very hard to hold back his tears. At this moment he remembered his grandmother's advice: "You must be brave in the face of unforeseen circumstances."

After he brushed his tears away, he went empty-handed into their igloo. His grandmother said nothing. She got up and left him there and went out to the tunnel porch. Within a few minutes she came in and called him into their yard. She took him to the path that led into the village and through it. She gave him two infant heads. "These are your juggling balls, Tutgarrluung, my dear Tutgaq. While I am singing a song, you juggle these heads as you walk all the way over to that last igloo. When you reach the other end of this path you must drop the balls on the ground. Are you ready now?"

"Aang, yes, grandmother," answered the orphan boy.

She sang her weird-sounding song. Then, the boy began to juggle the heads rhythmically. When he reached his destination he dropped them on the ground, and as soon as the balls hit the earth he heard a loud thudding sound of upheaval. At this moment a disastrous calamity occurred within the whole village. The orphan boy ran toward his grandmother, choking from inhaling dust. He reached their igloo and sat down nearby with his grandmother. His grandmother asked him one question which he never forgot. "Do you see," she said as she waved her hand over the shattered igloos, "what happens to people who refuse to be kind to the poor?"

He nodded and said, "Yes, grandmother." Then he leaned over to her for protection from shock which he needed at this very moment. They were the only survivors of the calamity and all but one igloo had overturned on its foundation.

His grandmother took his hand and led him toward their igloo.

At this point in the story one of the listeners would always ask the storyteller, "What did they eat for supper then?"

The storyteller would answer: "They had dried ug̃ruk meat and wild ptarmigan willow greens which the grandmother had preserved in seal oil, food to be eaten in those severe times of starvation or catastrophe that often occurred when our world was young. Akkamii, the story has ended."

A story had once more served its purpose. Since the ancient past, the Eskimos' environment has had dismal and hazardous conditions for living. The children were taught once more the need of being kind and considerate.

Ptarmigan Legend

There is a story about two Eskimo boys who abused a poor ptarmigan which one of them had caught in a snare. To abuse wildlife, even the game that is caught for food, is taboo in Eskimo culture; and, according to the teaching of tribal elders, he who does such an act of cruelty will be punished, one way or another.

Once two boys set out to check their snares in the wilderness. As they neared their row of snares, the younger boy saw a live ptarmigan caught in one of his snares. The bird was trying to escape, but the snare held it tightly by the leg.

"Look! I caught one!" the boy cried.

The two boys stood watching the bird as it lunged this way and that. Suddenly the younger boy had an idea. He said, "Say, I wonder what would happen if we plucked the feathers from it. Would it be able to fly?"

Both boys laughed at the possibility of an exciting experiment. The older brother said, "Let's do it."

"I'll hold it while you pull the feathers," said the younger one. And, together the two boys sat down to do the trick. They plucked feathers until the poor ptarmigan had none left except on its wings. Then they climbed a mound nearby to do the experiment.

Repeatedly they threw the bird up into the air, and repeatedly the bird would beat feebly with its wings and fall to the ground. The boys thought this was funny and laughed at the ptarmigan. When they had tired of their sport, they went on about their business of checking the rest of the snare line, and they left the ptarmigan to die where he had fallen to the ground. They did not go back and get the bird after they had checked all of the remaining empty snares. They were probably afraid to let their parents know what they had done to one of the wild creatures.

Several days later the boys returned to the place where they had carried out the experiment. They found only the feet of the bird. A fox had probably eaten the unfortunate creature.

Sometime later the younger boy became very ill, and soon after this his older brother was gripped by the same painful disease. The village shaman tried to cure them.

The shaman visited the miserable brothers every day to get information on whether the parents had carried out his prescriptions. Their main medicine was an herb tea, a very potent antidote for sickness. Sometimes he made them drink seal oil and red-tipped lichen. He would ask the spirit to answer his question whether the brothers would get well. This was done by placing a paddle under the patient's head, while silently asking the spirit a question. He explained, "If I lift the patient's head lightly, it will mean that he will get well; but, if I cannot lift his head with a paddle, it will mean that he will not get well."

Without speaking a word, the patients and their parents would know the prophecy by watching the shaman's attempts to lift the heads. The heads of these two patients were never lifted. This meant that they would have to suffer in bed and wait for death to relieve their painful existence.

Now the shaman admitted, "Their disease is incurable. They must have broken some taboo."

But the boys would not confess what they had done. They were ashamed. And so they lived on in their sickness, becoming old men in their misery. Finally, when he was dying, the older of the two called the shaman and told what he had done when they were still boys. But it was too late now; both men died miserable deaths.

Thus was fulfilled the maxim: "Silam Inua is everywhere. He knows when we mistreat either humans or animals."

But there are some people who do not admit the truth of the saying until it is too late.

Eskimo Shaman's Flight to the Moon

The blizzard had been ravaging the Eskimo village of Kotzebue for three or more weeks. The old man shaman had power to heal the sick, but he had no control over the storms. He was known to entice and be influenced by the workings of the good and evil spirits. He could not understand why he could not calm the violent windstorms. He and his people suffered from the effects of the cold every year. So, this particular night of violent windblasts, he felt sorry for the handicapped, widows, and orphans. He consoled himself by saying, "I hope the blizzard will soon subside. After the month of January, the sun will thaw the sunny side of my igloo. Then, I can enjoy its warmth as it penetrates my body. Sometimes it is unbearable, especially when we are short of firewood since we have to share it with the poor. When one is old, the cold creeps in, even to our innards. Then we are like a housefly and forced to hibernate in our igloos. It is amazing how the housefly survives in the cold."

At this moment he looked around the wooden rafters of his igloo, but he could hardly see them since the roof rafters were only partially lit by moonbeams. "What shall I do? I'm so cold. This old parka is worn out. I'll have to have another one made, also a caribou sleeping bag. This old one has lost its qiviut (down feathers)."

He could not sleep as he kept listening to the whistling and clattering sounds of the wind outside his igloo. He looked at his dog; it, too, was shivering, but still slept. He envied his dog's undisturbed rest. At this time he thought of the possibility of moving his people to a warmer place. Then his idea of searching for such a place sounded reasonable.

"I wonder if the moon is a place like our earth, and would it be a warmer and more pleasant place to live? But how can I move my community up there?"

There would be no harm in flying to the moon this very night instead of bearing this sleepless ordeal. He watched the moonbeams, though at times their rays were shadowed by the thick, rushing snow. He was inspired by its persistent peekings, like a light being turned off and on.

He got up, put on his clothing, and went out. He went over to his bench and sat down. From there he examined the moon's rugged surface and, after a time, he thought, "I might be able to land on the dark spots of the moon. They appear to be stable land formations."

He went back into his igloo and rekindled the charcoal; as the fire warmed his body, he began to sing as he usually did when he wished to talk with the earthly spirit. He said, "I will make a special effort to entice the food spirit by using my charms and the noise makers."

Within a short time, the spirit entered him, and once again he became a powerful shaman. At this moment, he presented his goals to the spirit. The spirit answered his questions and advised him to fly to the moon, giving him the following directions: "Leave your body in your sleeping bag. First, a deep sleep will come over you. It is at this time your spirit will fly away toward the moon and, as the spirit leaves your body, you will feel as if you have your body with you. This is the time you will lift yourself up light as a feather. Keep saying in your thoughts, 'To the moon I fly, to the moon I fly'."

The old shaman did accordingly, and soon he fell into a deep sleep. Then his spirit soared out of his igloo right through the window. Up, up, he swiftly travelled.

Zoom! Swish! Swish! He felt very light and did not feel cold or scared. He set a direct and vertical course toward the moon.

After a short period of flight, he landed on the pinnacle of a moon mountain. Then, as soon as he adjusted himself, he examined the surface of the land around him. He noticed that his surroundings, near and far, were a wasteland of rocky, black-colored peaks with hollow craters between them. He became morose and said, "Such a gloomy land. There are no birds, no vegetation, no lakes, no rivers, and no people."

He stood up and started to search for signs of humanity, or even animals. He did notice a valley which appeared to have a smooth surface on which he might walk. He was feeling chilly as he made his way toward it. When he finally reached the valley, there was a man coming toward him. It was someone he knew! "Nakin aggiqpich, Illuuq? Where did you come from?"

His friend pointed to the tallest mountain above them, "Pikunga, right up there."

"What a surprise! I didn't expect to see you up here. Mind you, we're on the moon, Illuuq. I got miserably chilled last night in my igloo and I couldn't sleep, so I decided to search for a warmer place to live. When I saw the moon, it appeared to me as a shining earth and I thought it would be such a comfortable place in which to live, and so I came up. What brought you here on such a night?"

"You know, I had the same idea about this beautiful moon. It was so cold at Point Hope and I felt sorry for my people. I decided to fly up here with the help of the good spirit. I am so disappointed. It is worse here. Down on our earth, at least the storms subside and give us time to enjoy the spring, summer, and fall, until the cold winter again arrives."

The Kotzebue shaman agreed with him. He accepted Illuuq's summation with, "Ammiuvva! That's right! Let's leave this old cold moon and fly back to our earth and homes where at least we'll have food and daylight. And later on in the month of Kusugaqturvik (February, meaning a month of melted snow droplets), the sun will begin to thaw the snow again."

After embracing happily, they parted and took off in the same direction toward the ball of earth beneath them. The old shaman from Kotzebue seemed to travel faster on his flight back to earth.

When he arrived, he went in through the window of his igloo. As his soul entered into his lifeless body, he muttered to himself, "My! This old flesh of mine is stiff and cold. But I must reactivate it, since I wish to live as long as I can."

He began to shiver uncontrollably; his teeth were now clattering so loudly that his dog began to bark at him. He got up very slowly to rekindle the charcoal in his fireplace, heated some water, and then drank some herb tea. He felt relieved, so he got into his sleeping bag to rest once again and to regain his normal body temperature. The dead feeling in his limbs immediately began to thaw away.

While the dawn was approaching over the whole village, he recalled his relationship with his friends and relatives: "I am glad my relatives did not come in while I was gone. They might have buried my old body. Then my soul may have had to wander around in this cold air outside."

He thought of the spirits, the good and bad influences over all the Eskimo shamans. He vowed to himself, "I will help my subjects faithfully hereafter." He fell asleep soundly as he thought of the feeling of warmth in the relationship to both man and the mother earth of which he was a part.

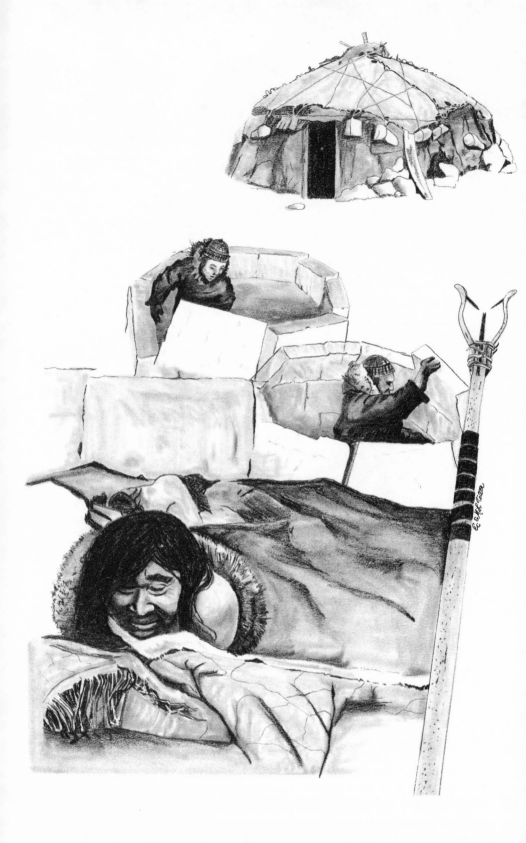

Snow Igloos and Sod Igloos, A Modern Tale

Two cheechakos, newcomers to Alaska, sat in a Fairbanks hotel lobby vehemently arguing. They did not notice an Eskimo woman sitting nearby.

Finally she walked over and asked if she could help settle their argument.

"How absurd! How can a snow igloo exist?" one cheechako asked. "Who would live in it? Do humans live in a house of snow? I can't picture myself actually living in a snow house. Why, it's impossible! The snow roof would melt if I were to build a fire for cooking. The snow roof would melt and drip all over the place. The bedding would be soaking wet in no time. And I would suffocate! A house without a window or a ventilator wouldn't have proper circulation. When I went to school, we were taught that such houses existed, but I haven't seen a snow igloo since I came here. All I can see in these Alaskan towns and cities are houses like ours. I wish that I could talk to someone who knows about snow igloos or read about them in Alaskan literature and prove that they do exist."

"Yes, there are snow igloos in arctic Alaska where it is cold," the Eskimo woman explained. "It is summer now, and the snow igloos have melted. If you wish to see one, come to Alaska in January. Take a flight on Wien Alaska Airlines. They will show you a snow igloo in the Arctic. The Inupiat," she explained, "also have sod igloos."

"My people are mysterious," the Eskimo woman continued. "They don't explain matters pertaining to their cultural customs and their

71

primitive living, but I am willing to do so. Snow igloos did exist, do exist, and always will exist as long as we Inupiat thrive."

"I wish that I could build a snow igloo. This is very interesting. How do the Inupiat keep the chunks of snow from breaking? I should think the snow would fall apart," the second cheechako said.

"The force of the high winds compacts the snow," the woman explained.

"And, if anything is frozen, it doesn't fall apart. So the snow igloo builder works with hard chunks of snow, piling one on top of the other."

"Do humans live in the snow igloos?" one cheechako asked.

"Yes," the Eskimo said. "Humans live in them when an emergency arises. For example, a snow igloo can be built immediately to serve as temporary protection against a blizzard which may last for days and days. Fifty years ago Eskimos used them for emergency obstetric hospitals. They were welcome abodes when mothers had to deliver their babies while travelling. The mothers stayed in the snow igloos until they were strong enough to continue to travel by dog team."

The two cheechakos leaned forward in their chairs and listened intently as she continued her explanation, "About seventy years ago the Inupiat didn't worry about their heating facilities; they used an Inupiaq lamp. The people stored prepared food to eat, such as dried and frozen fish and meat, seal liver, greens preserved in oil, and frozen berries.

"At the present time a hunter loads his sled with gas burners, lanterns, dog chains, and white man's food. He wastes valuable hunting time preparing his breakfast and drinking coffee instead of watching for game. In the old days an Inupiaq hunter rose early in the morning to hunt and was usually successful. He had only the oil lamp adding heat in the igloo; therefore, the interior of the snow igloo didn't drip. The only time the Inupiat use this type of an abode is in subzero weather. The interior of it will not melt and drip in 50 degrees below zero. The bedding doesn't get soaked. Furthermore, the Inupiat used damp-proof caribou sleeping bags in the old days. The present generation Eskimo hunter has an eider-down sleeping bag like yours.

So I don't feel sorry for people who use modern sleeping bags and get chilled when they sleep in the snow igloos.

"You said that you heard there are no windows in the snow igloo and you think that you would suffocate if you slept in one. Well, you're right this time. Snow igloos lack windows. There is no reason to have windows. An Inupiaq would waste his time if he tried to carry and install windows, since the snow igloos must be completed before nightfall. Furthermore, what will an Inupiaq see if he should look out the window? He would only get a glimpse of the vast snow-laden tundra."

"Well, how does the hunter get enough fresh air when he sleeps?" asked one of the men. "Does he put a vent somewhere in the snow igloo?"

The woman shook her head and said with a slight smile, "Now if you were camping out and the thermometer registered 60 degrees below zero, would you want a vent? Or would you just be satisfied to know that sufficient air was coming in the entrance? And the snow itself breathes unless it is insulated from the inside. By now, I hope you realize that snow igloos are only temporary. But my people have permanent dwellings, too. These are called sod igloos."

"Say!" exclaimed one cheechako to the other, "Do you suppose those sod igloos are anything like the 'old sod shanties on the plains' that are so much a part of our past?"

Then they both turned eagerly back to the woman as she went on to say, "Well, I wouldn't know about your kind of sod houses, but I'll tell you about ours, and you can draw your own conclusions. An igloo is built over a dugout in the ground. The roof and passageway are the only parts of the house which are built on top of the ground. Driftwood is used to make a four-cornered frame; in the north, where there is no driftwood, whale bones are used as substitutes. The next step is to place horizontal cross beams onto the frame. Then the builder starts on the dome-shaped roof which has a pole in the center. He places pieces of small driftwood or bones around the upright pole and leaning on the beams. To insulate it, the women collect dried grass and moss to place all over the log structure. The northern

Inupiat use caribou skins or hides instead of grass. They use one-square-foot cubes of dried topsoil or sod for the outside covering of the roof. This protects and preserves the igloo from the severe weather of northern Alaska. This structure has one window in the roof. In olden times the Inupiat had no glass, so they used dried ugruk (bearded seal) intestines sewn lengthwise. Now in the Arctic, some people use window glass, but this is not very practical since the glass breaks so easily.

"A sod igloo looks quite primitive on the outside, but when one enters the structure he can see that modern conveniences are being successfully adopted by the Native housewife. At Meade River, where I taught for two years, people lived in sod igloos. When I first came to the village, I noticed radio aerials on all the homes. I wasn't a bit surprised when I went inside and saw washing machines, modern stoves, and furniture being used."

"To get back to the original subject," put in one of the gentlemen, "How do they enter the house? Do they have a regular door?"

"No. Up to seventy years ago the Inupiat built tunnel porches so they could keep the heat in the house. They had to stoop to enter the low porches and small doors. Some houses still have them.

"In the spring, when it is time to leave the villages for seal hunting, the inhabitants tear off the roof and leave it open. They know that during the summer the sunshine will freshen the inside of the igloo. When they return, they rebuild the roof.

"Now, cheechakos, I hope that you have a clear picture of the two types of typical Inupiaq dwellings in Alaska: the snow igloo and the sod igloo."

After both men said they understood, the woman asked, "Just which one would you choose, if you were given a choice?"

They answered quickly, "The sod igloo! Not only does it sound more comfortable, but you know, it really sounds a lot like the sod shanties the pioneers of America built."

"Are there any more questions you'd like to ask?" the woman said before she turned to go.

"Oh, yes! Can you tell us why you were named 'Eskimo'? The dictionary defines the word as 'raw meat eaters.' It also states that you are 'a diminutive tribe, living in Greenland and Alaska'."

The woman stood silently for a moment before she answered, "The French Canadians named the Canadian Natives 'Eskimos.' So when the explorers from other countries travelled to Alaska, they called us that, too. In other words, they arbitrarily gave us the name. Our ancestors for many years called themselves Inupiat which means 'humans' or 'the real people.' The definition of the word Eskimo needs correction, according to our cultural standards. The writer of the dictionary referred to us a raw meat eaters. He didn't make himself clear to the reader. He gave the reader the impression that we eat fresh raw meat and fish. We don't! The northern Inupiat eat frozen food which has been stored for several months at a time. Some of your food is cured, too. Cheese is an example; it has been aged, so that people will like it. Your cheese must have a ripe flavor. We apply the same method in preserving and curing some of our food.

"Since we are on the subject of Eskimo food, will you allow me to correct some of the errors, or misinformation given to the public?"

"We'd be pleased," they replied, "and perhaps we can pass the word along in our travels."

"Eskimo ice cream is not an ice cream in our kitchens. It is a salad base, such as your salad dressing or mayonnaise. Eskimo ice cream is a mixture of caribou suet, seal oil, and water. No salt is added. The Eskimo housewife delights in preparing a dessert dish by mixing this base with fresh blueberries, salmonberries, cranberries, and blackberries. A little sugar is added sometimes. Wild, leafy greens, Eskimo potatoes, and other roots are also mixed in with the caribou mayonnaise separately. My mother taught me how to make the salad base, and I love it and will always like to eat it," the Inupiaq woman said proudly.

"We are much obliged for this informative conversation," one of the cheechakos said. "When we return to our homes we'll tell others what you've so kindly given us. By the way, who are you and what is your name?"

"I am an Inupiaq from Unalakleet. My name is Ticasuk. It means 'a hollow place in the ground'," answered the woman. "I am thankful that you gave me an opportunity to explain some of our ways of living. There is much more to tell, but I hope that I have made myself clear. I feel that I must act as a spokesman for the humble, peaceful Inupiaq who isn't bold enough to defend himself in the English language. My people's policy is 'Silence is the first step to humility.' I wish that I had their patience and humility. My boldness certainly doesn't portray an Inupiaq heritage. My part-Russian ancestry compels me to explore the white man's vast field of education. You ask who I am? Please, just say that I am an American."

Raven, a Great Hunter

Young Raven, as he was flying over the arctic coast, spotted another bird on the beach—an eider duck. As Raven landed and skidded nearer to the stranger, he said, "Hello, Lady Bird."

"Hello, Mr. Raven. I'll share my lunch with you."

"Thank you. I had a big breakfast this morning. In fact, I was searching for some seals which the high tide usually beaches on the shore."

"I'm a sea diver. My family subsists on shellfish, and you?"

"The sea mammals, and land animals as well. I'm a good hunter, Lady Bird. Isn't this a beautiful day up here? Do you have a family?"

"No, not yet. When I'm of age, Mamma said, I'll possibly have a family. How about you?"

"That's what my parents tell me, too."

They both laughed.

"If you gather a pile of shellfish, I can haul them for you and bury them under the sand on the beach for you."

"That's a very nice idea," she agreed, and added, "Please put a landmark near the mound, so I can find it easily."

Thereafter, they became companions for the rest of spring. Soon, the snow and ice melted; and, as it did, love for each other bloomed—and so suddenly! Then, one pleasant evening, young Raven asked a special question, "Will you be my wife? I'll help you when you build our nest."

79

And to his surprise, she accepted his proposal. Raven was so happy that he danced around his bride, the eider duck lady. From that day on, they lived together happily. Moreover, as he had promised, he was helpful to her and protected his family of five little ducklings. Three of them were brown like the mother, and the two male birds were identical to their father. They had black feathers and orange-colored claws.

As Mrs. Raven watched her children growing up, they continued to resemble their parents: the three ducklings looked and behaved like her, and the other two like their father. In the late fall, their children reached adulthood.

Some fowl migrate from the north to the south where it is warmer in climate. One cold day, Mrs. Raven explained to her children about the migration of some birds, "We cannot live in our summer homes when winter comes, children. If you wish to move away with me, you can follow me as I fly southward over the ocean. You see, your father lives up here all year, but I don't because it is too cold and the ocean freezes where I get my food. If all of you wish to fly with me, let me know this evening. We'll leave early tomorrow morning. Is that all right, Father?"

"Yes, the boys and I will have to decide. I think I'll just go along as far as I can, boys, and you can go along with Mama. You might freeze to death up here. Anyway, we'll all meet again to spend the summer here."

The children decided to fly south. Though their father felt bad, he did not show it. He said, "I'll fly with you above the coastline as far south as Tikiraq, Point Hope, which is on the peninsula on the Bering Strait."

"Yes, Dad," a son replied, "Mother and we children can spend a day and a night with you on the beach, eh boys?"

They all left next morning. It took them five hours to reach Tikiraq, where the Eskimos live.

During the evening, Father Raven said, "I will fly out to the ocean to say goodbye to my family, then return to the land."

This plan made his family feel happier.

PART II

Mr. Raven flew high over his family while they skirted the waves. He thought, "The rough sea makes me sick so I think I ought to return to the land."

He managed to yell loud enough to be heard by his family, "Goodbye Lady Bird and my sons and daughters."

In answer to their father, the Raven, they flapped their wings.

As soon as he left, he cried, and said, "To think that I'll spend the winter alone. Where will I live and with whom?"

He could not wipe his tears until he landed, so he decided to try to float on the surface of the sea. When he did, he began to sink, and the waves slapped him around every which way. "I wish a miracle would happen to me." And, sure enough, there appeared a great big door before him which said, "Come in, Mr. Raven, and dry yourself in my living room."

He felt relieved and hopped in. The door popped shut right behind him. "Oh! I am thankful for this lift."

The invisible owner who was leading Mr. Raven through the hallway said, "Sit here and rest, but please don't touch my lamp at the ceiling. If you do, you and I will be in darkness."

Raven promised he would not touch the lamp. He sat for a long while watching the blinking lamp. Then he asked himself, "Where am I, and why is this room so terribly dark?"

After a while, his curiosity got the best of him. He flew up to the lamp and poked at it several times with his bird knife which he had kept under his wing inside its case. All of a sudden, the light went out. When Raven went down, he bumped the floor very hard. In the darkness poor Raven began to rock back and forth from one side of the room to the other. And he smelled a putrid odor around him and his feet felt sticky. His wings were matted together. He could not breathe; he knew he was suffocating. "What shall I do?" he thought.

He began to cry and great teardrops washed his sticky face. Since he was very thirsty, he gulped these droplets and that made him feel a little cooler. When the house stopped rocking, he decided to cut an outlet through the wall with his knife. He worked very hard to cut a square opening in what he thought was a wooden wall, and every few minutes he would run his fingers through the slit he had made. He cut and cut and pushed and pushed and pushed.

As he pushed harder, the square began to move, and his repeated efforts made him feel stronger. When he pushed on the square piece for perhaps the hundredth time, it popped outward and he heard water splash as it landed outside. Light came streaming in and blinded him, so he leaned against this window. He did not know how long he stood there. Then he said, "Thank goodness I'm breathing fresh air into my lungs."

He felt his chest and it was like an inflated balloon. Now, Raven was able to peck very carefully through the porthole he had made. To his surprise, he saw a long beachline with its skirt spread out as if to receive the wavelets for herself from the sea.

Raven was so happy and wanted to smile, but he couldn't because his feathers had matted together and he couldn't move his facial skin. All he could do was to crow and crow until other land birds and sea birds began to fly around this house he was in.

He finally managed to jump out through the hole he had cut and, when he did, he plunged right into the shallow water of the beach. As he was bathing there, the wavelets turned red. Then he hopped farther up onto the dry sand and suddenly turned around. Do you know what he saw? A large animal! He did not know what he had done until that very minute. He had killed a big baleen whale. He said to himself, "I'm a good hunter, Lady Bird."

Akkamii! The end of the story.

Ihlliagaq's Big Haul

M any years ago an Eskimo boy, Ihlliagaq, lived with his grandmother in a house called an igloo. It was built on a ridge of the seashore. Its dome-shaped roof was like a giant mushroom and on this sat another little mushroom that was used for a window and vent. Directly underneath this vent, in the center of the interior of the igloo, was a fireplace. On the floor near the wall of the igloo was a trap door which opened upward when it was pushed. Out in the yard there was the entrance to the house, with a passageway built under the ground to the trap door that opened through the floor. Ihlliagaq and his grandmother lived in a semisubterranean dwelling.

One day, his grandmother took him down to the beach. Ihlliagaq noticed that the sea was very calm and that the tiny ripples were gently splashing on the seashore. When he and his grandmother arrived at the beach, she pointed in the direction of a long stretch of shoreline before them. She turned to ask him a challenging question, "If you walk on this beach you will find many kinds of fishes and possibly other animals, too. We need some fresh food. Do you think you can find some for us and bring them home today?"

"Yes, grandmother, I'll search until I find some," he answered with a big smile.

After she left, Ihlliagaq stood and listened to the coaxing sounds of the wavelets which seemed to be urging him to start walking. He noticed the long stretch of shoreline before him and marvelled at the distance he was about to travel. And, as he was walking, he came to a tomcod which was alive. He muttered to himself, "Oh, I know what to do. I'll just swallow all I find."

Then, at this moment he could not resist saying a rhythmic lyric:

"Ahytygtul' luku
Caniqiirturlaku
Igkaku
Brush all the fins off
Before you swallow fish
Then swallow gently
So they won't go squish!"

So he took the tomcod, washed it in salt water, brushed off the fins, and swallowed it whole. Since he did not chew the fish, it slid down easily. After walking farther, he found many other fishes. He found trout, a whitefish, a humpback, a dog salmon, and a big king salmon. He swallowed each one, and they all tasted scrumptious. He walked slowly now, very carefully, because his stomach had swelled up and had become heavier.

As he walked farther on, he found a crab. Distastefully, he watched it while it was crawling away. He whispered to himself, "I won't eat this one. It will be harder to swallow, I'm sure. He has too many legs and bones."

He watched it as it disappeared into the deep sea. He left. While he was walking, he thought to himself, "The fish I've swallowed is not enough for a whole winter's supply of food, so I will continue to search for other types of animals."

Before very long, he came to a baby seal. He took its whiskers off, washed it, and swallowed it whole. As soon as he stood up, he noticed the baby seal's mother nearby. He walked over, cut off its whiskers, washed it, and swallowed the whole big seal. Ihlliagaq had to rest for a while before he walked farther. As he did so, he saw some bigger animals up ahead. He counted them: a baby ugʳuk and its mother, a baby beluga and its mother. After he swallowed each one he could not move nor walk because his stomach was too heavy. It had enlarged and now had reached the gravel under his feet. He said, "What shall I do to lift it up so I can walk home?"

Ihlliagaq pondered for a while about how he could move under such a terrific weight. Then he had an idea which he knew would work. He said, "I will lift the far end of my stomach and place it over my shoulder."

He exerted all his strength to do this task, and he was successful. His next move was toward the higher ridge, above the beach. Perhaps, he thought, he could find a freshwater pond and drink water, for he was very thirsty. He found a pond not very far from the ridge, so he drank all the water in the pond.

"Now that I am much heavier than ever before, how am I going home?" He stood there and planned, but not for very long, "Oh, I have an idea. I'll walk back to the shoreline."

There at the waterline he went into the deeper sea and dropped his stomach on the water. It did not sink. Instead, it floated gently and, as he swayed back and forth, it seemed weightless. "Now," he said happily, "in this manner, I can tow my big haul all the way home."

As he started walking knee-deep in the surf he sang his little song:

> "Brush all the fins off
> Before you swallow fish
> Then swallow gently
> So they won't go squish!"

Arriving in front of his home, he simply lifted his stomach to his shoulder and walked up to his house. However, he walked very carefully and slowly for fear of puncturing his swishy-swashy abdomen. When he finally arrived at the main entrance, he could not enter—he was too large. So he climbed the dome-shaped roof until he reached the gut window and there he called to his grandmother, "Grandmother, please let me in."

"Come in through the window."

"I can't. The window is too small and I am too big."

His grandmother ordered him to wait awhile out there. Poor Ihlliagaq began to feel insecure for the first time since he had left home that morning.

All of a sudden a bellowing order came from within the house, "Come in through the eye of my old needle."

Ihlliagaq was surprised that he, of all children, could slide through the needle's eye. As he was sliding through, he felt relieved and he marvelled at his grandmother's big idea. His grandmother directed him to sit down near the fireplace, but not too close.

"Whew! Grandmother, I am cold."

"Sit closer to the fireplace, then."

He sat down as close to the fireplace as he could. When he eventually got too warm, he took his parka off. This move exposed his abdomen. At this moment his grandmother warned him again, "Ihlliagaq, look out for the flying sparks. They might lodge on your stomach and burn it open."

Just then, while she was speaking, a hot, burning charcoal flew directly toward him, and sure enough, it nestled right on his navel. What a catastrophic flood followed! His stomach split wide open, and the animals made horrible gurgling sounds while they surrounded him and his grandmother. All of the fish and seals he had eaten and all of the water he drank drained out until their igloo was flooded almost to the rim of the window. Since the animals were yet alive, they began to churn and turn in a circle. At this moment, Ihlliagaq spotted his grandmother and her wooden platters and a ladle bobbing up and down on the surface of the water. What a sight! "I'll have to rescue her."

So he swam over and grabbed his grandmother and pulled her up into a platter with all his might. Then he climbed in too and, sitting behind her, used the ladle to paddle out through the gut window. They landed safe and sound on top of their igloo, but they were miserably wet.

"Now, we have enough food for a whole winter," she said. "Ihlliagaq, I am proud of you! We will invite our relatives and have a feast and dance to the gods of our animal kingdom."

Ihlliagaq felt relieved and happy.

His grandmother pointed to the outside entrance and said, "Go down there, enter through the tunnel, and push the trap door wide open so that the water will drain out the floor of the igloo."

"Oh, what a relief!" she said to herself.

After he had gone, the old lady smiled as she thought of her grandchild's unique way of hauling his heavy and enormous catch.

A teacher who reads this ancient Unaliq story to school children should point out to them that the grandmother's purpose in sending out Ihlliagaq was to teach him to think for himself. This he did, by improvising—using his stomach as a carrier and using the water to float the load.

Yonge and the Flounder

Yonge was an Eskimo boy who was just six years old. One day as he was walking home from the river where he had been watching some of his older friends fishing for tomcod, he thought to himself, "Now that I am six years old, it is time that I learned to fish. Then I can go out with my friends to the ice holes. I know I am big enough to land a fish. I will ask my mother if I could go fishing for tomcod tomorrow."

He became so excited thinking of the fish he would catch that he ran the rest of the way to his home. As he burst through the door he called "Aakaang, Mother, may I please go fishing tomorrow? If you let me use our tomcod hook, I promise not to lose it or bend it, and I promise not to get the line tangled. Please, Mother, may I?"

His mother smiled and said, "Yes, Yonge, you may go if you promise to be careful. Don't let anyone else play with the hook and remember how your father showed you how to jiggle the hook on the river bottom to attract Mr. Tomcod.

"Call your father for supper now. You must go to bed as soon as you have eaten. You will have to get up early in the morning, for Mr. Tomcod is an early riser who floats in with the first tide."

Yonge was so excited that he did not go to sleep for a long time. When he finally fell asleep, he dreamed that he caught twenty tomcods and he ate them all.

His mother awakened him early the next morning, and he ate his breakfast as fast as he could; he was so anxious to start fishing. He carried his hook and line in a skin bag his own size. Yonge went out of the house and he had to blink his eyes because the sun was so bright on the snow. "Oh, what a beautiful day for fishing," he said to himself.

Yonge stood on a snowbank and looked toward the river. He spied a fisherman jigging for tomcod. Yonge said, "I will join him and we will fish together for tomcod."

In a few minutes he reached the river and saw that there already was a hole chopped through the ice near the other fisherman. The hole was so inviting that it seemed to say "Come, Yonge. Drop your hook right here. There are lots of fish just waiting to be caught."

Yonge asked the other fisherman if he could fish there.

"Ii-i, yes," replied the fisherman. "There are enough fish for both of us."

Yonge carefully dropped his hook and line through the hole until he felt the hook hit the bottom of the river. Then he sat down and began to jiggle his hook just as his father had taught him. All of a sudden something was pulling on his line! Yonge let out a yell and hurriedly wound up his line. Soon he was pulling a struggling fish out of the water onto the ice. But what was this? This fish wasn't a tomcod. Yonge was very disappointed.

Then the other fisherman said, "Don't be sad, Yonge. That fish is a very good fish."

"But what kind of fish is this? He is so flat and round. I did so want to catch a tomcod."

"That fish is a naatarnaq," answered the fisherman. "It is a flounder. Take him home to show your father and mother. They will be very proud of you."

Yonge was eager to show his parents the fish he had caught, even if it wasn't a tomcod. As he skipped along toward home he sang a song to himself about his great adventure.

Yonge's mother and father thought that the flounder was a wonderful fish. Yonge went back to fish again and again; and, of course, he caught many tomcods after that.

Johnny Niuqsik, Squirrel Hunter

Johnny Niuqsik and his grandmother were out in the hills; they were hunting for squirrels in the spring. Johnny's first day of hunting was exciting. He helped his grandmother pitch the tent, and he thought it was fun to chop the spruce branches. He carried them inside the tent where Mrs. Niuqsik laid them on the ground. The branches were used for the tent floor. Mrs. Niuqsik and Johnny would sleep on the branches.

The work was done. The tent was up. The beds were made. The stove was ready for its fire. Firewood was piled in back of it. Johnny wanted his grandmother to tell him a story.

"Grandmother, please tell me a story," he coaxed "How did you and Grandfather hunt squirrels? Did you have a camping outfit? Did you have a tent? Did you have a stove? Did you have sleeping bags like ours?"

"No," answered Grandmother, "we did not have a camping outfit. We had no tent. We had no stove. But we had warm bedding. It was called muukuluk. It is a sleeping bag made of caribou skins."

"Tell me, Grandmother, where did you sleep? Did you sleep under a tree?" asked Johnny.

"If you will listen, I will tell you about it. When I get through, we will skin some squirrels. Will you help me?" His grandmother looked at him and smiled.

"I will, Grandmother," promised Johnny, "I will."

95

"All right. I will tell you a story. When the time drew near for hunting squirrels, your grandfather and I mended the snares," said Grandmother. "We also mended the bow and arrows. I twisted the whale sinew for him. We used twisted sinew instead of twine. We had no guns to kill the animals. We had no traps. Bows and arrows were used to kill large animals, and we used small snares to catch squirrels."

Johnny asked, "What kinds of large animals did Grandfather kill?"

"He killed caribou, bear, eagles, mountain sheep, and wolves. He also killed foxes, wolverine, and lynx. The furs were used for parka trimming," Grandmother answered. "Boys were taught how to use the bow and arrow. They went hunting with their fathers. They had to be brave."

Johnny nodded. He knew about being brave. "Go on, Grandmother. Tell me some more."

"Well, I will tell you how we travelled. We travelled by dogteam. We used only three or five dogs to pull the sled—it was better to take fewer dogs, because we did not want to waste dog food. Our camping outfit was light. Eskimos were kind to their working dogs: the people never rode on the sled but walked along with the team. We had trained leader dogs. The leaders were trained to turn to right and left."

Johnny asked another question. "Grandmother, how did you go up the mountain?"

"We followed the river," answered the grandmother. "We travelled as far as we could, to the end of the river. Then we climbed the mountain and camped in the edge of the forest. Your grandfather always knew the safest place to camp."

"How did you build your igloo?" Johnny asked.

Grandmother said, "Our igloo was made of tall willows, grass, moss and branches. First, snow was cleared away until the ground was bare, then willows tied at the tips were placed upright in a circle. These tall willows made the igloo frame. Then the igloo was covered with grass. At last, it was covered with branches and hard snow." Grandmother smiled and said, "How would you like to sleep in an igloo, Johnny?"

"I think it would be fun, Grandmother, but how did you keep warm? How did you cook your food?"

"We had warm bedding. We had warm clothing. We wore fur parkas and fur boots. We had no camping stove, but we knew how to build a fire. It was very simple. When you strike two flint rocks together, sparks fly out. The sparks set fire to dry grass and twigs. You must learn how to start a fire, Johnny," Grandmother told him.

"Yes, Grandmother, I will try. Will you show me?" Johnny asked eagerly. Then, before Grandmother could answer, the boy asked, "May I go out hunting with you tomorrow? I would like to learn how to set snares."

Grandmother laughed. "Yes," she answered, "you may go with me tomorrow to set snares. Now, I think you and I should skin these squirrels. Then I will boil the squirrel meat and we will eat it for our supper."

"If I catch enough squirrels, will you make a parka for me?" asked Johnny.

"Yes, I will make a parka for you. You will have to take good care of a squirrel parka. The skins are not very strong. They tear easily. Shall we skin these squirrels now, Johnny?" asked Grandmother.

"Yes! Yes, Grandmother," shouted Johnny.

"I am glad that you are interested," said Grandmother. "I hope that you will become a great Eskimo hunter. Then you will be a village helper. You can help others learn to hunt."

Uğruk Hunters

Uğruk is a bearded seal. It is the king of all the hair seals. Eskimo hunters risk their lives to hunt it.

The uğruk lives on the moving ice. Hunters must wear special snowshoes to walk on this thin ice. They must crawl very slowly and carefully. They wear fur mittens and kneecaps; fur slides easily on the ice. The hunters wear snowshoe hare or white cloth parkas for camouflage. In olden days, seals were hunted with harpoons. Today most of the hunting is with rifles.

Before a hunter attacks an uğruk, he makes sure it is asleep. While he is crawling toward it, the hunter stops if it lifts its head. If it is asleep, he crawls to it. When he is close enough, he will shoot. All these rules an Eskimo boy must learn.

Eskimo hunters must look and listen, and they must know many things. If the wind is blowing offshore, it means open water. If the wind is blowing toward the land, it means no open water. In the evening a hunter studies the sky. If there is a large ring around the moon, it means storm. If he sees a sun dog in the direction of the winds, he is glad. He knows what kind of weather he will have in the morning.

One day two members of an Eskimo family were talking. They were Mr. and Mrs. Niuqsik. They were talking about hunting. "Mother," said Mr. Niuqsik, "tomorrow morning I am going hunting. It is time to hunt for uğruk. Our son Johnny will go with me. This will be his first hunting lesson. Will you fill our lunch boxes? Will you fill my hunting bag? Be sure you put the things we will need in my hunting bag. Johnny must go to bed early tonight."

Mother was happy to hear this. She was glad that Johnny would learn to be a hunter. She said, "Yes, Father. I'll call Johnny now and tell him. I am sure he will be very happy to go. How good ugřuk meat will taste again! I know you'll bring one home."

Mother told Johnny about the hunt. He was very excited. He said, "I will go to bed early. I will do everything I can to become a good hunter."

When Johnny had gone to bed, Father sharpened his knives. The knives would be needed to cut the seal he killed. Father cleaned the guns carefully, and he gathered all the things they would need for their hunting.

Early in the morning, Johnny was awakened. He dressed quickly in his hunting clothes. He ate his breakfast and was ready to help his father.

After breakfast Johnny carried the things to the sled. His father loaded the sled and covered it with a canvas. The sled load must be tied carefully. The snowshoes, guns, and harpoons were placed on the load where they would be handy to get when they were needed. The hunting bag filled with hunting clothes was tied on the load. A kayak sled was fastened to the big sled. The kayak, an enclosed boat covered with ugřuk skin, is used to drag the seal to the main ice. The kayak sled, complete with kayak, is fastened to the main sled with a rope, like a trailer.

"Johnny, lay out the tow line and tie it to the sled," Father said. "We'll use only eight dogs today. Harness the lead dog first. Skippy knows how to lead the others wisely, and he holds the tow line while we harness the others."

"Yes, Dad," answered Johnny.

The dogs were jumping and barking loudly. This made it hard for Johnny to put their harnesses on. At last they were hitched. Father took his foot off the brake, and he and Johnny started on their journey.

Father Niuqsik and Johnny travelled toward the frozen sea. It was cold, but Johnny enjoyed the ride. On and on the dogs pulled the sled. They knew how to follow the unmarked trail. Their ears listened for animal noises, their noses smelled animal scent. They travelled very fast.

"Do you see the edge of the main ice, Johnny?" asked Father.

"Yes, Dad, I see the thick ice floes and the thin ice. The thin ice looks gray. The ice floes look white. Is this where the uǧruk lives?"

"That's right, Johnny. We'll have to leave our dogs here. Whoa, Skippy! Johnny, unhook their harnesses and lines. Work fast. I'll tie Skippy to the post and get the kayak sled. We'll pull the sled to the edge of the ice."

The dogs rolled around in the snow, gleefully. Some licked their paws. Others ate some snow. They were thirsty and the snow slaked their thirst. It was time to leave them. Now, both the man and the boy were off to hunt.

As they were pulling the kayak sled, Mr. Niuqsik gave Johnny his first lesson. "Johnny," he said, "we learn by listening and watching. Hunters should not talk loud. Loud talking scares the animals away. I will put on my white hunting clothes. You put on your hunting clothes, too. Uǧruk hunters must look like icebergs."

After Father and Johnny put on their hunting clothes, Father said, "Now we'll sit and watch for uǧruk, when they come up through the ice to breathe. If they get close enough, I'll shoot. If I kill one, it will float. You'll have to get my kayak quickly. Then, I'll harpoon it from my kayak and tow it slowly to the main ice. You may get the dog team. The dog team can pull the uǧruk on the ice. Do you think you can remember what I've told you?"

"I'll try, Dad," said Johnny.

"Sh! Sh! An uǧruk is coming toward us. As it comes up for breath, I'll shoot it," Father whispered.

"S-w-i-s-h!" The uǧruk came up through the thin ice. Mr. Niuqsik's shot rang through the air. It hit something. Johnny gave a yell. As the uǧruk circled in the water, it began to float. It was dead. Johnny ran to get the kayak. His father got into the kayak and paddled swiftly. When he came near the uǧruk, he hurled his harpoon through the air. As it struck the uǧruk, Mr. Niuqsik uncoiled the rope from the shuttle. He tied the other end of the rope to the kayak and began paddling toward the main ice, pulling the ugřuk with him. There was also a float, an inflated seal poke, which was tied to the rope near the harpoon to provide extra flotation and identification if the ugřuk had to be left for awhile and thus would not be lost.

"Oh, boy!" cried Johnny. "We'll have some fresh meat." He laughed and talked to himself as he ran for the dog team.

When Johnny reached the scene of the killing, the dog team helped drag the big ugřuk onto the ice. Johnny smiled at his father.

"Johnny, bring my hunting bag," said Father. He took off his hunting clothes and packed them carefully into his bag. He kept talking, "Johnny, we're going to skin the ugřuk now. We'll have to hurry. Will you bring my knife, please. Bring your knife, too. You"ll sit and watch me as I skin it. Be very careful. Don't cut your fingers. The knife is sharp. After I cut open the front part, you may begin. The flippers must be taken off."

Mr. Niuqsik slashed the blubber next to the meat. Then, he gave his knife to Johnny. Johnny learned fast. They took the skin and the blubber off. The next step would be to clean the ugřuk out. Johnny watched his father as he cut the seal apart. After placing a canvas on the sled, Father called Johnny to help him pack the ugřuk skin. It was very heavy. They placed it on top of the canvas and then carefully packed the meat in it. They folded the ugřuk skin and the canvas over the meat, then tied it all to the sled.

Father smiled at his son. "Now we're ready to go home, Johnny," he said. "Be sure to put on your warm clothing. It is going to be cold. We have a heavy load. If you run with the dog team, it will help to keep you warm."

Johnny hitched the dogs once again, and they travelled home following their earlier tracks. How happy Johnny's mother would be! As Johnny ran along with the team, he whistled a tune with glee.

Forgetful Eskimo Boy

One time a little Eskimo boy took a walk on the main ice near the beach. While he was walking on the edge of a lead, a wide and long crack in the ice, he saw a tomcod in the water. He did not know that the fish could float until he saw it. Then he asked the fish, "What is your name, fishy?"

It answered, "Ayagghsramik ata pikia, call me Ayagghsra."

"Oh, I will go home and tell my mama that your name is Ayagghsra. I'll keep saying it, so I won't forget it as I run."

So he started to run home pronouncing its name. But before he left the ice, he fell down and forgot its name. He went back to the fish and said, "What did you say your name is?"

It said, "Ayagghsra."

He promised the tomcod that he would not forget it this time.

The tomcod said to him, "Don't run too fast, then you won't fall down."

Then the boy ran very carefully and as he entered his house he pronounced the fish's name loudly: "Ayagghsra!"

And his family answered him very loudly, "Ayagghsra!"

And that is how the little Eskimo boy learned how not to forget new words and names.

Akkamii, I'm finished telling the story.

Curious Little Mouse

Field mice live underneath the grasses. In a particular mouse village lived a mother mouse and her family. The new baby born in their burrow home was now big enough to peek out at the big outdoors for the first time.

As a baby mouse peeked out of her burrow one day, she saw tall trees outside of their door. She said to herself, "Oh my! I wonder what's above the blue sky. And these tall trees must be holding up the sky."

Then she thought about it and said, "I am going to find out. I will gnaw the trunk of this tall tree that is holding up the sky."

She worked very hard, until her jaws were tired, because she was just a little mouse. As she was gnawing away, the tree seemed to sway back and forth. And when it was swaying toward her, she would run into the tunnel and listen. That day the tree did not fall. She went to sleep thinking about the tree that was still standing, the beautiful blue sky, and other trees she had to gnaw.

When she awoke, she said to her parents, "Mom and Dad, I am going to make the blue sky fall today."

Her parents answered, "Go ahead, that's the only way you will find out, little Mousie."

She went outdoors and watched the clouds, birds, and flies. The she began to gnaw the tree that held the sky up.

And all of a sudden, the tree fell, and shook the earth where she was. Then it was too late to run into the tunnel.

"Oh, my! I am so glad the tree and the sky didn't fall on me."

Actually the "tree" was just a large stalk of grass, but that is how a curious little mouse found out that the grass-stalk tree did not hold up the sky.

Miraculous Little Seal Poke

O nce the Island brothers, Little Diomede and Big Diomede, lived separately, and yet not too far apart; a mere distance of three and one-half miles was the expanse of sea that separated their parallel shores in the Bering Strait. Their main villages were situated on each island at their south terminal jut of land. There were two brothers that lived on the islands. The younger brother, Nukaqhliq, and his family of four children and his wife, lived on Little Diomede Island, which is now in American territory. His older brother, Angayukhliq, and his childless wife lived on Big Diomede Island, which is now within the Russian boundaries.

Angayukhliq was a successful hunter who supported his people of the Big Diomede community. On the other hand, his younger brother was not as skilled nor determined, and sometimes he and his family depended on Angayukhliq's supply of food. Eventually Angayukhliq's wife resented her sister-in-law and her frequent visits, especially during the darkest and coldest months of the year when the seal hunters ceased to hunt on the ice. Furthermore, only the hardiest men went hunting in the hazardous weather which could last for many, many days.

They searched for the seal in his special place of habitation. The male seal lives in his own special place: a continuously open hole in the ice pack, in the crack where the ice would push and break open. He comes up to breathe in the air and to find a place to rest himself.

It was during the bleakest part of the year that Angayukhliq's younger brother became seriously ill and very soon after died. Then Angayukhliq offered to support Nukaqhliq's wife and her small children. During the same year, and during the coldest weather, the Little Diomede people exhausted their food supply. The strong and terrible winds and cold blizzards caused the permanent ice to break up, and when the ice left, the sealeries drifted away with it. The absence of game birds and small land animals deprived the people of a valuable food source and promised nothing but starvation for them. Nukaqhliq's wife searched and searched for ptarmigan or other small animals, but she finally had to turn to her brother-in-law's house for food. The daily portions from his wife became smaller and smaller, however.

One day she trekked across her now familiar trail to Big Diomede Island. As she entered her relatives' igloo, her sister-in-law reported, "My husband has been unlucky this past week. Every time he brings home a seal, our people beg for part of it for their food. I really don't have much food to give to you!"

Nukaqhliq's wife then sat down by their doorway, at least to get some rest and thus renew her strength before making the long trip back to her home. It was at this moment her hostess went out, and when she came back in she announced, "I set your bag in the tunnel porch; you can pick it up as you leave."

"Quyaana! Thank you!"

When she lifted her bag it felt much heavier. She thought, "She must have given me more food this time. I am thankful. Oh! I am so fortunate to have my husband's brother and his wife to help us. If they didn't supply us with food, we could starve to death."

Then she came to a spot on the trail were the strong tides had made a huge ice mound. She climbed to the top and sat down for a rest. Then, she felt hungry, and this hunger nagged at her so much, she finally gave in to her desire to eat at least some meat and blubber. She sat still for a moment, then opened the bag to get some food. But what she took out of the bag were three slate rocks. She stood them upright upon the mound. "Well," she said, "so this is why my pack was so much heavier!"

She covered her cold face with her hands and began to cry and wail, like the wail of the wind the storm had given to her back. "This crying is a sign of weakness!" she scolded herself, "I must find my way home. My children will miss me."

Then she resumed her way bravely.

While she was walking across the bay on the ice, the strong winds swirled a mass of snow up off the ground and filled the air with a heavy whiteness. Since she was blinded and could not follow her usual trail, she began to crawl. While she was crawling, she suddenly came to a door. Curious, cold, and weary, she entered. She was so exhausted and breathless that she just sat by the entrance. All of a sudden, she saw a streak of light overhead. Someone spoke to her: "Oh! Yah! Come into our igloo. You must be very cold!"

A lady smiled to her in welcome. Her husband asked the young woman, "How did you get here?"

Then she told him about her plight: her disappointments and the dilemma of being so lost. Then he said, "You can stay with us as long as you wish, or until the storm is over."

She managed to thank him, but at this same moment, the wife began to portray a scene: "How beautiful it is to see a couple of snipes both searching for food on the morning of a beautiful spring day, as they hop along the beach happily, just as my husband and I did after we were married!"

"Hush!" her husband said to her. "This is no time to be telling stories. This woman needs help. Get some food for her so she can gain back her strength!"

She went out, and within a short period of time she brought dried ug̊ruk meat and seal oil. While eating this food, Nukaqhliq's wife was grateful. Then the host related instructions to his wife to fulfill immediately: "Go to the sirluaq, the underground cellar, and bring a tiny seal poke which has been prepared with survival food."

Then he directed his attention to the widow who by now had finished eating her food, and he instructed her how to carry the seal poke, "You must carry the little seal poke in the palm of your hand in an upright position. Don't drop it, and when you reach your igloo, lay the little poke first in the sirluaq and again lay it down on a flat rock on which a straw mat has been placed. Leave it there until the morn-ing, and when you take some food from it, don't be careless—try not to spill oil on the floor. You will see what will happen."

Before the widow left her kind friends, his wife laid the little seal poke in her mittened hand and said to her, "Carry it in this manner until you reach your destination."

The widow left after she thanked them.

When she went out, she noticed that the storm had subsided, as well as the fact that the sun had gone down. She said to herself, "I must walk as fast as I can. My children must be very hungry."

She kept guarding the little seal poke, so that she would not drop it accidentally.

When she arrived home, she followed the directions in the manner the man had given. Her attention was drawn strongly to her home conditions, the starvation, the devastation of a once hardy Eskimo people. Before she left the sirluaq, she kneeled on the rock and poured out her needs to Silam Inua, the Owner of the Universe.

"Grant my request," she prayed, "Oh, Silam Inua, let it become a large seal poke, so that our people will survive. Grant that the animals will come back to us."

When she got up, an idea came to her: "Why not gather little pieces of animal skins of every kind and spread them out in the tundra of your islands?"

She then said to herself, "Tomorrow, I shall do this and see what will happen."

She went into her igloo very quietly so she would not wake her children. "I'm glad they're asleep. It helps to take away the hunger pains."

She was so tired, she did not undress but took time only to take off her worn-out mukluks. She slept very lightly, and before the children stirred, she went out very carefully, hurried to the sirluaq, and entered it. To her surprise, she beheld a huge seal poke bulging with enough food for her people. She rushed to her igloo and, taking the largest wooden pan with her, rushed back to the sirluaq and the miraculous seal poke. As she was digging for the precious and delicious food of every kind, she was careful not to spill any drops of oil on the floor. As soon as she returned to her igloo, her children woke up in time to see the platter full of food. One of them said, "Aakaang! Mother, who gave us this good food?"

"A miraculous seal poke," she replied.

And while they were eating, she told them about her experience the day before. But she was careful not to mention the unkind treatment her sister-in-law had given her.

The rest of the day was spent collecting small pieces of skins of land animals. When she thought that every kind of animal was represented, she went out to the tundra to place them on the land. When she laid the skins on the tundra, she would whisper a wish, "I hope you'll become a real animal by this spring."

When she went home, she brought food to each home. From that day until spring, she supported the village people with part of her survival food. The children's strength was replenished and they were able to play outdoors.

One day, their uncle came to visit his brother's wife and his nephews. To his profound surprise, he found them in good health. He asked his sister-in-law, "How did you manage to keep alive?"

She related to him the experiences she had. She told about the gift of rocks instead of food she had received from his wife, where she left them to prove her statement, the storm which caused her to get lost, and finally how she received the little miraculous seal poke by which the people of the Little Diomede Island were saved from starvation.

Her brother-in-law's reaction when he heard about his wife's cruel act made him very angry, and he said to his sister-in-law, "She'll get her reward."

Then he went home following the trail between Little Diomede and Big Diomede islands. When he came to the ice hill on which Nukaqhliq's wife said she had placed the rocks, he found the three pieces of slate which his wife had given her in place of the much-needed food for the young, starving children. While he was walking back to his home, he planned her punishment.

As soon as he entered his igloo, his wife invited him to eat his supper. He said, "I'm troubled and I'm not hungry."

"What happened?" she asked him.

"I found the three slate rocks you gave to that helpless woman instead of the food which she asked for. That is what happened!"

His wife dropped her head down and became fearful. Without saying another word, her husband brought three slate rocks and then laid these before her and reprimanded her, "You can live on these rocks the rest of your life."

With this final statement, he left her and went back to his brother's house and family. While he was walking, he said to himself, "I will teach my nephews how to hunt skillfully."

For the rest of the spring days, his brother's wife received many animal skins from the people she had saved from starvation. She would ask the hunters whenever they brought in a skin of a wolf, wolverine, or caribou, "Where did you acquire so many skins of these animals?"

The hunters would ask her in a reflective way, "Didn't you spread the animal skins over the wilderness with a wish for a miracle to happen, so that the animals would return to us? Didn't you desire our hunger to be gone and our clothing needs to be answered?"

Then she would just smile, a genuine smile to show her grateful spirit.

A Legend: On How to Exchange Gifts

O nce in the animal world, an exhausted walrus surfaced
once more, presumably to inhale some air and float. As he
tried to float, he kept sinking, so he floundered about in the
sea. "Why can't I float like a whale?" he complained.

At this moment the old walrus saw a beckoning beach, a peaceful
place on the shore. "I will swim to the shore; there I will lay this bulk
of mine to rest," the walrus said.

So he plunged "kaplunk" into the deep. Then he set his flippers and
crawled on the ledge-like table where the sea water bathes the coast.
"I'll lie down here. Oh! It is so restful to feel the cool water spray on
me. I shouldn't have eaten so much, but I'll survive and feel more
energetic after I sleep. I'm glad no one else is around!"

No sooner had he closed his eyes than he heard a whirring sound
above him. "Hello, Mr. Walrus. Are you all right?"

"Of course, Mrs. Ptarmigan, I'm just trying to rest," he replied,
trying very hard to be pleasant as he spoke. He really was disgusted
with her. He smiled awkwardly at this intruder.

"Do you sleep on the surface of the water sometimes?"

"No! I've wished many times that I had been provided with such a
device that would let me float on the water." He blinked his eyes
slowly, implying a hint, "You know what I mean, don't you?"

"Yes, Mr. Walrus, you can have my crop. I don't need it because I
travel in the air. If you place my crop under your chin or in your neck,
it will make you float; then you don't have to swim ashore to sleep.

You are in danger here, Mr. Walrus. The bear might kill you, for he runs faster than you do."

"That's a good idea and you're very kind to me. Wait a minute. I'll give you some of my sharp claws, Mrs. Ptarmigan. Put them on right away. You will be able to dig faster as you make your bed in the hard snow." This time the walrus smiled at her brightly as he handed the claws to her.

"Thank you, Mr. Walrus, and goodbye."

After the lady ptarmigan left, the walrus split his neck wide open and placed the crop into his neck and sewed the skin together. Then, of course, a miracle happened right away. The slit healed while he was asleep that afternoon.

"Now," he said to himself, "I'll go home. And when I get tired, I'll rest as I float."

From that day on, all the walruses obtained floating devices on the sides of their necks. But at this time, the old walrus thought he was the only one to have received a floater.

Legend of Kotzebue Village
Angilararnailaq

PART I

An Eskimo family was travelling northward in their umiak, each person taking a turn paddling. They moved slowly along, hugging the shoreline. It had been an adventurous trip since they had left their home in search for an ideal place to settle. The observant father, alert for signs of game, steered the skin boat into every cove along the shore. The dusky shadows of late evening reminded them that soon they should camp. The tidal currents seemed to help the boat drift faster to their destination. The currents took them toward the mouth of a river in the lowlands. "It will soon be dark," the father announced as he turned the boat toward a landing.

His wife and boys smiled approvingly and began to paddle faster. They knew in the morning that they would explore the new countryside.

While his family made camp, the father set the fish net out in the sea. So, then they sat down to enjoy the beautiful scenery across the bay. Low purple mountains were reflecting their color on the glassy water as the sunset faded away.

After supper they retired, agreeing that this would be their future homesite. The parents knew they would find an abundance of wild game to hunt on both land and sea.

In the morning their net caught many fish. It was the beginning of a successful hunt. There were many caribou, fowl, and fur-bearing animals. Lakes were full of fish. The sea swarmed with ugřuk, whale, and

123

spotted seals. Berries, roots and edible greens were plentiful. Every day they gathered food until they had to build storage caches called sirluaq. They gathered driftwood to build their igloo. It was satisfying to move into a warm igloo, knowing that they had a house and an ample supply of food for the winter.

Toward spring, other families arrived. They were welcomed; it was good to see other people. The residents shared their food with them and encouraged them to live there permanently.

Now there were many families living in the new settlement. Other travellers were made welcome. Soon the friendly little village became a large community.

They lived peaceably and contentedly in their village. Nature's storehouse provided them fresh water from a river called Kangiq. This river flowed into a large lagoon where fishes were plentiful. Beluga whale and seal were speared from the hunters' kayaks as they skillfully maneuvered in the lagoon.

One evening, one of the hunters reported to the chief that he saw a strange creature in the lagoon. He described it to the chief excitedly, "It looks like a woman with beautiful long hair. I'm sure it is a dangerous mermaid."

The chief didn't believe the report until one of the hunters was lost there. The chief of the Kangirmiut gave an order to his people to leave the lagoon and to search for another hunting ground where they would not be molested.

Early one morning, a hunter reported to the chief that he found an ideal place to hunt. He excitedly pointed to the place, "There are many spotted seals there. It isn't very far from here. It is located at the mouth of the river where there are two outlets and a delta between them. The delta is completely surrounded by water and it appears to be a mating place of spotted seals."

The chief was pleased to hear the good news. He called a meeting to announce the discovery, and he said, "The elders will give you advice as to how the seals can be killed."

Then he sat down to listen to the elders. A spokesman advised them, "In your kayaks, you should quietly approach the seals while they are asleep. Abandon your kayaks on the beach and crawl until you are near enough to see their eyes, then stand up, form a circle, and join hands. Each man must be ready to snare the seals when the alarm is given. As they escape toward the sea, you can snare them. The hunter who found this place will lead you to the new hunting grounds tomorrow morning."

PART II

Since the Eskimo's livelihood is wrought by capturing wild animals which often leads to dangerous adventures, the people highly honor a great hunter. However, in every community, jealousy among the people breeds contempt.

At Kangirmiut, a young man named Nailaq became the best hunter. His younger brother named Angil acquired the same hunting skills, and he also was destined to become a great hunter. Like some proud people of the world, the older brother was a boaster. He claimed that he was the only good hunter in this village, and, as he was becoming very popular, he pictured himself ruling the people as their future chief. But the fate of some proud people sometimes is misfortune.

Among the young hunters, there sprang up one almost overnight who was considered even mightier than these two brothers. The people turned their hero worship to this new young man, and thus ended the popularity of their former idols. There was only one solution— murder!

The people of Kangirmiut found their latest idol murdered, the first such crime committed in their midst. The leaders conferred immediately, only to be informed that the murderers had left the village with their families.

This was the beginning of a separation from the first community. A neighboring village was settled overnight. It was named Kangiq after the freshwater river nearby.

Living as fugitives was not a happy life for the two brothers. In order to protect themselves and their families, they decided to encompass the village they had deserted. The younger brother was given an eastern post as a fort (now known as Lockhart Point). Nailaq ordered his younger brother to kill every hunter who came to hunt seal at the sound: "Use any method to annihilate travellers. I will use my own skills and methods. We'll rule over the sea and land. No man who enters into our midst will ever return alive."

After Angil departed to settle in his new post, Nailaq took to the nearby plateau where he could make plans. He had heard of a lake where a dragon lived and decided to go there. As he was nearing the lake, he stopped on the edge of a grassy stream. "Ah," he said as he gazed across the lake, "this is the dragon lake, the home of a dangerous walking serpent." As he stood in the grass, he felt a strange feeling creeping upward from his feet. He knew he was about to find something to punish the people he had left. He glanced down to his feet and saw a beautiful striped baby dragon. It seemed to say to him, "I'll help you, take me, my mother is asleep in our house."

He gathered grasses and rubbed them together to make soft bedding for his new pet. As he took the dragon into his hands, he vowed he would take good care of it. "I will feed it with my own food," Nailaq said to himself.

When he got home he placed it in an oblong wooden bucket and took care of it for a whole winter. The pet dragon grew until he completely coiled around the bucket.

Toward spring his younger brother, Angil, visited him and saw the pet dragon. It was now too large to live in a bucket, so the brothers planned to build an igloo for it. Since no one knew of the dragon's existence at Kangirmiut, they built its igloo under the high bank, very skillfully and quietly. It was large and made exactly like their own. Nailaq thanked his younger brother for helping him to build the dragon's igloo.

One evening as the younger brother was making preparations to leave for his home, Nailaq asked, "May I go with you tomorrow and visit your new fort? I would like you to show me how you plan to kill the travellers."

"You are invited to come with me tomorrow, and you shall see my post."

They left very early the following morning. As they were nearing his fort Nailaq said, "Stop the team. I'll not go near your house. I see two polar bears standing on either side of your entrance!"

"Now you know how I kill the travellers. They never return home. My pet polar bears kill them," responded the younger brother.

On his way home Nailaq came to the new road which led toward the village of Kangirmiut. He was glad he walked home. Now he knew which way the people travelled. He must plan a way to stop the use of the road.

The pet dragon had the best of care during the year in its new home. Nailaq hired two servants to take care of this pet which continued to grow round and round the interior of its igloo.

One day the servants reported to their master that the dragon's many legs had disappeared and only four were left. He could walk on four legs! Within a few days, the master ordered the servants to train the dragon to walk in and out of its igloo. "This must be done during the night. I don't want anyone to see the dragon!" he commanded.

When it became a full-grown dragon, it could follow the guides in and out of the igloo. Every day the dragon consumed an enormous amount of food. Nailaq, the proud master of the monster dragon, would tell it about his plan to kill the people. It seemed to understand. Since the dragon could lift a seal in its jaws, its master knew it could easily lift a man.

One late evening, a stranger came to their igloo. He had just arrived from a distant village. Nailaq ordered his servants to give the stranger choice food to eat. He didn't know it was to be his last meal!

Nailaq's revenge would become a reality this night. He felt relieved that at last he could feed humans to his pet. And this man's death would prove to them that the mightiest hunter was in their midst. "Go and fetch my pet dragon," commanded Nailaq.

In a short while, the poor stranger heard stumping sounds coming around the igloo. The servants came running through the entrance and hid. The poor stranger was doomed. While the man was sitting on the floor the dragon's head with its strong jaws reached quickly for him and gulped him down.

"Now take the dragon back to his igloo," said the master.

Year after year Nailaq's pet dragon killed many travellers from the neighboring villages. Angil and Nailaq, the two dreaded enemies of the interior Eskimos who wanted in vain to hunt for the sea animals, reigned as the watchmen of the sea.

PART III

Eskimo hunters of the interior villages were concerned over the disappearances of their sea hunters. Certainly there must be a brave man among the villagers, at least one to attempt to solve the mystery.

This mystery set a young man to thinking. Napariaq, a brave young hunter, thought about the two idols he was wearing concealed in a necklace around his neck. He thought to himself, "I know I can rely on my idols, a tuft of down and a mink skin." He reached for them and said as he examined both, "Shall we fight for our people's rights of hunting?"

He must help his people. He must do away with the barriers of selfishness and jealousy, the result of which was becoming evident. Famine toward spring meant death through starvation. Sea animals supplied them everything for their existence: shelter, tools, clothing, and food. He would try to find a way to do away with the monarchs of the sea.

He resolved, "I must find a way."

Late one evening, he discussed his plan with his young wife. She would help him. They quietly made preparations for the dangerous trip which both would undertake with cunning in the early morning.

When they reached Itivyaaq, the portage to Kangirmiut, they changed their course and travelled on the coastline toward the large peninsula called Tikirayuatchiaq or Pipe's Spit. Napariaq knew they would enter Kangirmiut from the northeast. When they arrived at Tikirayuatchiaq, he announced to his wife, "Here we'll rest, then we'll travel on to our destination."

When they arrived at the smaller peninsula, Napariaq gave orders to his wife, "You wait here. I will now make an attempt to fulfill our mission."

To make sure he had his idols handy, he placed both around his neck. His wife was a brave woman, and she had faith in her husband's ingenuity. She smiled when he bade her goodbye and said, "I'll be back."

When he climbed over the peak, he saw smoke circling straight up from Angil's fort. He saw the two polar bears guarding the entrance of their master's igloo. He walked down to the beach and observed the condition of the snow. The snow within the high bank was soft and the outer part had crusted to make a hard surface, which was ideal for him to travel through as a mink.

So he took one of his idols and commanded it to change him into a mink: he immediately became that animal. Then he followed a course under the snow toward the guarded igloo. As he was nearing the igloo, the polar bear guards stood up, knowing an enemy was near at hand. Napariaq knew he had failed. What must he do now? As he stopped to plan, he thought of his other idol, the tuft of down. Napariaq, still as an animal, had to crawl further away and commanded his idol to change him to the tuft of down.

When he became the down, he was blown by a breeze over the snow toward the guarded fort. By now, the polar bear guards were asleep, each tied to a post on either side of the igloo entrance. As he was nearing the entrance, he saw a spruce pole that he knew he could use as a weapon. At last he now had the power to do away with the first barrier, and he could secretly destroy the enemy which plagued his people.

The down changed at once to a strong human warrior who stood at the entrance of the tunnel porch of the igloo. He used the spruce pole to kill the polar bear guards, first the right one and then the left. There was not one sound as he struck death to each bear.

He now planned to kill the master of the bears. The only possible way would be to do it with a bow and arrow from the top window, which was open. As he peeked in carefully and noiselessly, he saw his target warming himself near the coals of the smothered fire. Napariaq aimed his deadly arrow at the man who was singing a song while his aged father was listening nearby.

When the arrow went into Angil's back, he jumped up and tore down the rafters of the igloo, then dropped on the coals of the fire. His aged father died the same way.

Napariaq walked back to his wife. He felt assured that none of these happenings were witnessed by anyone from the neighboring village which he and his wife would soon visit. As he was walking away from Angil's igloo, he thanked his idol, the tuft of down, for making it possible to destroy the northeastern fort.

It was almost dark when they entered the council house at the village of Kangirmiut. The Eskimos were dancing. No one noticed them until someone shouted, "Iglaat, strangers!"

The people were surprised. Napariaq was questioned by the men as to how he and his wife had escaped from being killed. He answered all the questions and quieted them by saying, "Perhaps they were asleep and didn't see us, for we passed the igloo way out on the sea."

The next day toward evening, a little orphan boy was playing outside alone. Napariaq questioned him very carefully about the people who lived with the dragon pet.

Napariaq and his wife met alone. Again he confided his plans to his wife, "I'm going tomorrow evening to fulfill the second part of our plans. You know what to expect. Be sure to leave my parka inside the sled and hang the sled securely under the cache so the dogs won't tear my parka apart. Leave a small opening in the parka. Examine it secretly every day, and when you feel me in it, you can bring me food and water at night. Don't let anyone know you're caring for me while I'm living in my parka."

It was hard for the wife to part from her husband; she again must suffer anxiety alone, wondering if he were safe. She wished that she, too, could go along, but Napariaq must go alone on this great mission for his people. He had faith in his only help: his idol, the mink.

When the people of the village had gone to the council house to dance, he bade his wife goodbye, not knowing when he would see her again. He was brave as he quietly walked toward the dreaded dragon village. When he reached the village, he went to the igloo where he knew the dragon lived. He quietly crawled through the tunnel porch and peeked through the skin door. There he saw a huge coiled dragon, apparently asleep. The dragon took a breath and Napariaq saw the flexible skin heaving on its scaly neck. This would be the place to knife the dragon. Napariaq quietly made his knife ready for the attack, and then he plunged the weapon through the dragon's neck, trying to sever the jugular vein.

The Kangiq people were in their council house having a good time dancing. They didn't hear the thunder-like commotion the dragon made coiling and uncoiling in an attempt to save its life. Napariaq, after making sure the monster was dead, entered the council house of the Kangiq village residents.

No one noticed him until he asked for a drink of water. Nailaq, the master of the monster, was informed of the arrival of an iglaaq. He ordered his people to stop dancing immediately. They all knew that this stranger would soon die—they didn't know the dragon was dead.

Nailaq gave an order to give this stranger a feast, and his servants brought the choicest fare. He ate to his content, since he knew he was a deserving man. When he was given his last drink of water, Nailaq ordered his two servants to get his pet. Napariaq didn't show any signs of excitement, but he felt confident that he wouldn't be fed to the pet.

People waited to hear the thudding sound of the dragon. Instead, two excited servants rushed in and reported that the dragon was dead. There was a gasping sound from the master and the people. They didn't believe the servants' report of the dragon's death.

"How could this happen?" asked Nailaq, the master of the dragon.

The men showed the bloody soles of their feet and their bloody tracks as proof that the dragon was dead. Anger arose! Nailaq ordered that the mother of the dragon be brought from the lake.

Napariaq thought that he was doomed. He had made a mistake; he should have killed the dragon's mother first. But it was too late now, servants had already gone to get it. The people were doomed, but they waited. Napariaq made plans quickly while they were waiting. He talked to his idol, the mink, to give him strength to overcome his predicament. He made sure that his knife was secure and within his reach on the belt. The people were so curious and eager to witness the newcomer devoured by the dragon that they were unaware of their own fate.

Soon they heard the familiar thudding sound of the mother dragon's steps as she neared the council house. The servants rushed in and hid aloft, under the rafters. Napariaq was alert and in a position to grab Nailaq first. When the dragon's jaws and head entered the house, Napariaq grabbed Nailaq and threw him into the monster's mouth. The people yelled for help which never came.

This was the beginning of a massacre by the dragon. Because of Napariaq's strength, which he used to grab the people, they were all devoured. Soon it would be his turn to be eaten, but not in human form. He asked his idol to change him into an animal. The instant he turned into a mink, he slid quickly down the dragon's throat and with his knife killed the dragon from within.

Then Napariaq escaped safely out into the world through the rectum. He walked to the lagoon, where he could take a good bath.

Napariaq, still a mink, immediately plunged into the water and washed himself. Then he ate some food to strengthen himself while he rested in a hideout for several days. He knew it would take a long time, possibly several years, before he again changed into a man. He remembered the plans he had made with his wife. It was comforting to know that some day he would again live peaceably and safely with his family. Their enemies were now dead.

PART IV

Napariaq, who was now an animal, travelled along one moonlit night toward the village where his wife was waiting for him. He was thankful that at last home was near. Not even a dog was in sight as he climbed into his sled and inside his warm parka. The passing of time didn't matter much to him now; he was safely settled in his new home. He slept very comfortably during the night. This was the beginning of his hibernation.

His wife took care of him for a whole year. She was very kind and patient with her animal husband.

One evening when she went out to feed him, she found that he had changed into a year-old infant. She was comforted and knew he would soon become a man and live with her again someday.

As time went on, another man courted her and wanted to marry. She confided this problem to her infant husband. He said to her, "I can't hunt for you anymore, and you and I must have food to sustain us. You can marry him so he can take care of us. Someday I will return to you."

She considered his request, and she married the young hunter. He took good care of her and she in return made many beautiful clothes for him. One late evening when she and her second husband were lounging leisurely in their igloo, a man entered. He was a stranger to the husband, but not to her.

"Welcome, and sit down, my wife will give you some food to eat," the husband said, as he gestured with his hands for her to carry out his wishes.

She didn't move but sat with a smile on her face. She finally spoke to her second husband, "This is my former husband, a hero, who has risked his life to kill both of our enemies, Angil and Nailaq."

Without any comment, her second husband gathered his personal belongings and peaceably walked out of their igloo.

It was a happy reunion for Napariaq and his wife. They lived an undisturbed life with the descendants of the first settlers of Kangirmiut, the ancestors of the Qikiqtarřungmiut, the People of Kotzebue.

This was the hardest story I've done. When you listen to the storyteller in Eskimo, it is interesting. When you translate and write it into a white man's story, the original story becomes as if it were food with no salt. This story was told to me by Abe Lincoln of Kotzebue.

The original Eskimo village was destroyed when the Civil Aeronautics Administration site was built. The river northeast of the village gradually formed a delta, which in time became the area where the Kotzebue business section is now located. The southwest mouth of the river ran between the homes of Cyrus Adams and Arthur Field. The northeastern outlet was between the homes of Jerry Coppack and Herbert Norton.

The first settlers named this island Qikiqtar̆ruk. It is the rightful name of the village, not Kotzebue as it was later named in honor of the explorer. The history authors stated that Capt. Otto Van Kotzebue named the sound after himself.

One of the oldest Natives here, Abraham Lincoln, stated that his grandmother remembered stories about the strange people who came and visited them. He said his grandmother told him that the Native women mended Capt. Kotzebue's ship's sails, and sewed four ugr̆uk skins together to replace the torn one. Abraham Lincoln was proud to report this to me, although this was never mentioned in the written histories of his village.